The Warrior's Mindset!

By Ryan Felman

The cover of this book was created by Garrett Dailey, of Aion Media Co. You can reach him on Twitter @Libera_Rex and @AionMediaCo

First Edition

A product of Path to Manliness LLC

To my sons, I hope these words inspire you to live a fulfilling life.

Previous works by Ryan Felman

Reclaim Your Manhood

Path to Manliness Vol. 1

Gumroad Ebooks

The Path to Journaling

The Path to Twitter Dominance

The Path to Brand Management

Contents

Adopt the Warrior Mindset

Ryan Felman

Adopt the Warrior Mindset

Foreword

Society Needs Warriors to Step Up

When the barbarians are at the gate, suddenly masculinity isn't so toxic. In the western world today, most of us have it so good that we forget what true problems are. The easier modern life gets, the smaller our problems become. And the louder small problems appear. We once sought to fly to the moon and crush communism. Now we don't know how to rebuild our crumbling infrastructure of water pipes and bridges, and we fear gluten in our food.

"All that is necessary for evil to triumph is that good men do nothing."

- *Edmund Burke*

There's a culture war being waged right now in Western Civilization. A war that will decide the fate of the world that influences our children's upbringing. Yet, despite such great stakes, most men say nothing. They keep their heads down, as they were indoctrinated by 12 years of schoolteachers telling impressionable young minds how to obey. Western Civilization needs warriors to step up.

About ten years ago while driving an hour a day commuting for work, I listened to Adam Carolla's audiobook In Fifty Years We'll All Be Chicks. In this book he warned of how modern society was progressively getting softer and weaker. Discarding common sense in favor of safety nets and excessive regulations by a government seeking more control over citizens' daily lives. At the time, his book was touted as alarmist and ignored. A lot can happen in ten years when good men keep quiet.

First off, there can be no argument that society has grown softer over the last couple decades under the guise of progressiveness. We once fought mastodons and harsh winters with no technological aids other than spears and fire. Now we shelter our young from peanuts and trigger words. Much of human interaction today involves pushing buttons or staring at screens. Elon Musk might have been right when he said that humans are the biological bootloader of the machine world.

People once engaged in heated discussions to fight over the survival of the best ideas. Today we retreat into our safe little reality tunnels, surrounded by yes men who stifle any notion of confrontation. We say we want to be a united people, but the social media algorithms systematically produce tribes that rarely, if ever, interact with another. They cordon themselves off from anyone who might attack their precious beliefs. This is how we revert to believing in a flat earth. Every man on Earth has a camera on them. Where's the fucking cliff into the void of space?! Post that shit on Instagram!

Silicon Valley is a massive part of the problem. They've created a class-based techno-society. On Twitter there is the privileged blue checkmark class that receives special treatment and a disproportionately louder voice. Beneath them, there are the plebeians who are forced to fight for scraps of engagement. The giants of Silicon Valley seek to control the context of human discourse and it is through algorithms, hoodies and learning to code that they can control the future of Western Civilization.

And as more men lose their jobs at the factory, jobs they were trained to do from 1st grade to graduation, the tone-deaf techno elitists simply scoff at their plight saying, "learn to code." Yet if the roles were reversed and coders were forced to assemble the Tesla they covet so much or even change a fucking tire, they'd be as lost and hopeless as the truck driver who can't so much as read Qbasic. The divide between the techno class and the manufacturing class has never been greater. They may as well be from two different planets.

In Ray Bradbury's Fahrenheit 451, firefighters are called to burn books in their dystopian alternate future. By destroying all works of literature, the truth of firefighters of the past stopping fires rather than donning flamethrowers to burn such great works of art is lost. This truth is literally incomprehensible to Guy Montag, the book's protagonist. He is caught in an echo chamber crafted on a massive scale.

Books are records of the truth of our history and he who controls the present, controls the past. He who controls the past, controls the future. And as we see the techno elite of Silicon Valley wrap their coding fingers around the modern-day public square of social media, they are creating the context that suits their vision for an ideal world. Today's algorithms are the Fahrenheit 451 firefighters of the digital world.

Those who are guilty of wrongful thinking are wiped clean from the digital public square, despite what your first amendment right may guarantee. It gets worse. This creates a rippling effect that leads to the masses self-censoring for fear of being canceled themselves. You know it's true. You have found yourself erasing your thoughts out of fear. I too have decided, it wouldn't be safe to share that thought. I might get reported and banned.

There isn't much that can be done to combat being banned or censored on social media. Hope is not lost though. Recently, older forms of social networks have seen a resurgence. Blogging and email have both made a massive comeback in recent years. And it is cheap to do this yourself. Men who are sick of watching the decline and doing nothing, now have a voice to inspire untold number of men who are lost and disillusioned.

Through writing on a blog, you can stand up and fight against the decline of honor, masculinity and truth. Nearly two years ago, I started writing on PathToManliness.com. At first it was merely an outlet for my frustrations at a world that was distancing itself from reality day by day. Now it has become a platform for thousands of men to be inspired every month. And that number continues to grow.

During the 2016 election, there was a term that kept getting brought up, but is now an afterthought. "The Silent Majority." This stuck with me. As I've traveled around this great country, I notice that the traditional and sensible types are often found in that silent majority. They rarely speak up and are often shouted down by mobs when they do. Social media makes it especially easy to shout down a voice that you don't agree with. And most of these people are too busy raising their families or working jobs (often multiple jobs) to concern themselves with social issues online.

The very nature of the mainstream news, the internet and particularly social media is designed to reward those who spark outrage. And what sparks outrage more than unconventional, controversial or outright insane ideas. To speak up and say that a man should love a woman, raise kids together, and stick to traditional roles is not as exciting as the stories of identity politics, school shootings or sex scandals. In the battle of order vs. chaos, the internet industrial outrage machine craves chaos, even if order reigns for most of the real world.

Social Media is the Digital Battlefield for Our Souls

Our malls are dying, and with it our real-world public square. The mall rats of the 80s and even the 90s are a dying breed. A few malls struggle to stay alive, but they are no longer the communal gathering for teens and adults they once were. Gone are the days of meeting up with friends at the food court and pumping quarters into the arcade machines, they've been traded in for free prime shipping. Where we once spent Friday nights picking out a movie at the local Blockbuster, we now sit on our couch scrolling through an endless digital selection of movies and shows on Netflix. The internet is no longer the place for nerds to retreat to. It has become the modern-day social gathering for the masses.

This means that whoever controls the context online controls the course of culture, social norms, and the ability to spin whichever truth suits the victor. History is written by the victors. Social media has already become the battlefield for everything from what becomes culturally acceptable to swaying public opinion on social issue to the moral justification of real-world battlefields.

Social media has become the ultimate battlefield of ideas and this narrative warfare will only become more prevalent in the future. More and more people are being raised thinking social media is normal as it has been a part of their lives since birth. With less public places to congregate in, it only makes sense that people will spend more time online.

One battle that is being waged now is the narrative push to frame traditional masculinity as so called "toxic masculinity". Obviously, there are actions taken by men that are toxic in their nature. But to lump in all of masculinity with a few bad actors is to throw out the baby with the bathwater.

Toxic masculinity is an attack against traditional men. This is a PSYOP or psychological operation to divide the public using a vague term that is essentially a placeholder for whatever the audience decides as "toxic." This can mean anything from truly toxic behavior like being violent to more mundane, non-issues like "manspreading."

To combat toxic masculinity while shouting "The future is female" is truly toxic behavior. How are young men or boys supposed to interpret this divisive behavior? This is particularly damning when many men today are struggling.

For the first time in the history of civilization, there are more women in the workforce than men. This should surprise no one since more women have been graduating college than men. In 2017, 56% of students on campuses across America were women, and this trend is expected to rise.[13] By 2026, that number is expected to hit 57%.[13]

Social activists push a micronarrative about gender neutral bathrooms, while more significant issues that affect many more people are swept under the rug. Men are often seen as expendable. They are blamed as oppressors even when they are a minority today in colleges.

Schools teach boys to be quiet and to blindly obey authority. Often when men do speak up about real world issues, they are told to man up, or to "deal with it". At the same time, men are lambasted for not being open with their emotions or sharing their problems. It seems that much of society wants men to open up and connect with their emotional side... until they actually do.

How does a man stand up to the insanity that is being preached today? With so many men growing up without fathers, or with poor role models in their fathers, it has never been more essential for these young men to find the right path. And as a man who's navigated many common trouble spots that young men face, I feel it is my responsibility to show a path forward.

Simply sharing your opinions when young impressionable minds are being brainwashed by nonsense is a rebellious act.

The world wants you to be a degenerate.

The world wants you to be distracted.

The world wants you to be a drunk.

The world wants you to be fat.

Rebel.

A Place for Men

"Waste no time arguing about what a good man should be. Be one."

-Marcus Aurelius

Living your life with the mindset of a warrior will reinvent the way you see the world and the way that you see yourself.

In an increasingly soft and feminized society, there are many loud voices that are arguing that traditional, masculine men are no longer necessary.

But they're wrong. There is still a place for men in modern society. People think that men are no longer necessary in the comforts of modern society, that they are expendable, and young men everywhere are buying into these lies. These lies are affecting young men. One in seven young men between the age of 16 and 24 experiences depression and anxiety each year.

And who can blame them? They are beaten down and berated for the crimes of other psychos. They are told not to judge people, not to stereotype, not to be racist against a group of people. Most men are none of these things. Yet young men are demonized routinely. Their spaces to escape and act like men are routinely invaded by women who want to tell them how to act.

Men who feel lost give into to nihilism. They abandon more meaningful pursuits because they feel their life doesn't matter. So, they spend their days in a virtual world with video games and online forums. They spend their nights numbing themselves with alcohol and drugs. This all creates a negative feedback loop that makes your life feel even more insignificant, so you dive deeper into this dull and listless life. Eventually you begin to hate yourself.

You don't have to live like this. You can strive for more. You can learn to love your life. You can learn to love yourself.

Back in November of 2019, I had the fortune of being able to spend a weekend in a cabin on a mountain with an extraordinary group of men. These men are all highly intelligent, driven by purpose and they are all writers in some sense of the word. Every single one of these men left a profound influence on me. This brotherhood is one of the most essential aspects of male life that is missing from men today.

By forming a tribe of men or brotherhood, you will be inspired to live up to the standards that these men set forth in their own lives. A rising tide lifts all ships. These men will keep you strong when life can make you feel weak. These men will serve as a powerful network of references, opportunities and collaborators.

These men will hold you accountable and make sure you stay on the right path.

The problem with the modern world is the average person is content to only discuss simple topics. Most conversations are restricted to pop politics, sports and pop culture references. The average person is merely regurgitating other people's talking points, rather than forming their own ideas. Some can't even form their own opinion but merely follow those of someone with whom they agree.

Now that's not to say that there is anything wrong with sports or pop culture, but there is a longing for a deeper and more interesting conversation among most people. This is self-evident when you notice the rise of popularity in podcasts where they focus on long form discussion over one-liners and short soundbites. The era of television is giving way to the era of the internet.

Ryan Felman

1. Change Your Mindset, Change Your Life

Men are lost in modern society and have no role models, so they try to fit in by being consumers and corporate monkeys. It is only after we've lost everything, that we are free to do anything. Men are providers by nature, and modern society has robbed us of our purpose.

Men need a purpose. Men need a mission. The modern warrior knows his future self and is constantly driven by his mission. Too many men today are driven by the fruits of labors yet to be seen so they find themselves frustrated. They want the girls, the cash and the lambos but they don't want to do the work required first. Or they find themselves lost on how to achieve their mission.

How do you work towards your future self? Write down your goals. Write down the actual steps to accomplish these goals. If you feel your goals are lofty and unattainable, break them down into smaller, more reasonable daily tasks. If you can persist in these tasks every day, your goals will suddenly seem feasible. Most people overestimate what they can accomplish in a day and underestimate what they can accomplish in a year.

The modern warrior has powerful mental awareness. How does one achieve mental awareness? You need to solidify your priorities. Take the time to address your anxieties; identify all mental and emotional challenges that are obstructing your path. Much of this comes down to mindset; this requires change. Address each one of these issues, and you can change your life. The process of self-improvement never ends. A true warrior knows this. Adopt the warrior's mindset.

Life is all about building new neuropathways. That's the secret to mastering everything. And most people would rather say "I can't" than accept that they can change everything they want if only they spent enough time and energy focused on changing.

- **Solidify your priorities.** A man who hasn't designed his own set of guiding principles is a man who is at the mercy of his base impulses, or worse, another man's principles. I constantly harp on the importance of having a purpose, and many people don't know how to find their purpose. You can't be given a purpose. You must craft your own purpose; we will discuss how to do this in chapter 15: Craft Your Principles to Guide Your Life.

- **Address your anxieties.** It is more common than you think to feel anxious or insecure. To rise above your anxieties, you must confront the root of your problems;

go to war against your anxieties. For example, do you fear public speaking because of people staring at you? Is that because of what you are speaking about? Or are you that worried about other's opinions of you?

- **Stop worrying over what people will think about your actions.** Most people won't even remember or pay attention. The real problem is that you need to get these people to stare at you, because most are addicted to their phones. Maybe you aren't confident in your own body and you need to drop a few pounds to feel more comfortable in front of a crowd.

- **Identify all mental and emotional challenge holding you back from greatness.** You're destined for greatness, but your hedonistic pleasures are distracting you from your mission. Video games are giving you a false sense of accomplishment. Alcohol is keeping you from being fully present and alert. You will die one day, but you procrastinate as though you will live forever. We will discuss all of these in greater detail in Chapter 12: Voluntary Discomfort.

In Reclaim Your Manhood, the first chapter discussed the importance of hitting the gym.

This is because the gym can completely reframe your mindset.

The gym does more than just hone the body. It builds self-esteem, presence and a mindset that tells you that you were born to crush your obstacles.

Reclaim your manhood!

The gym doesn't care about your political affiliation.

The gym doesn't care about your sexual preference.

The gym doesn't care about your gender preference.

The gym doesn't care about your fucking pronouns.

All it cares about is the hours you give. The sweat you leave. The gym has no patience for bullshit.

Be fearsome. Be unstoppable. Be the man that no one wants to go up against. Adopt the warrior's mindset. When you have this mentality, the energy you give off is palpable. People will treat you differently. This is why you often hear sayings such as "fake it 'til you make it." But it can also empower you to believe in yourself.

Mindset is often underappreciated; the power of a strong mindset can push you past limits and help you achieve your goals. Be confident in yourself – if you don't, no one else will be confident in you.

"The dominant male, with his upright and confident posture, not only gets the prime real estate and easiest access to the best hunting grounds. He also gets all the girls. It is exponentially more worthwhile to be successful, if you are a lobster, and male."

– Jordan B. Peterson

Stand Up Straight with Your Shoulders Back

There is a reason why this is rule number 1 in Jordan B. Peterson's 12 Rules for Life. Having a winner's mindset is powerful and it will seep into all areas of your life.

Conversely, your life will be poisoned if you have a weak mindset.

Standing up with your shoulders straight is a powerful concept. It shows others that you are capable, whether you truly are or whether you are simply bluffing. Who is a thief more likely to target? The self-assured man walking confidently or the frail man with his shoulders down and his eyes meekly fixed on the ground?

If you want to be successful in life, you must have a strong sense of self-belief; self-doubt is holding you back from greatness. Quit letting the fear of failing infiltrate your mindset.

So, what if you fail? Everyone does. Learn from it and move on. We'll go deeper on how failure can help you in Chapter 14: How Failure Makes You A Stronger Warrior. To be able to take criticism and use it to refine your path is a superpower.

Adopt the warrior's mindset. Train to become harder to kill. Sharpen your mind. Hone your skills through real world practice. And form your band of brothers. You want greatness? THEN TAKE IT!

2. How to Adopt the Warrior's Mindset

Imagine that one day, someone is going to kill you, or at least try to. Now, imagine that he's not coming for one year. How would you spend your time during that year? Adopt the warrior's mindset for your own path to manliness.

The ancient Spartans devoted their entire lives to becoming better warriors. Sparta's entire civilization hinged on their ability to defend their homeland from foreign invaders. These men did what was necessary to ensure the survival of their way of life and today, we still talk about them for their actions echo in eternity.

So, how can you affect your odds to favor the outcome in this potential battle? How can you make yourself a better warrior? You must adopt the warrior's mindset.

How does one adopt the warrior's mindset?

Train in martial arts

Why bother training in a martial art when you can carry a gun? Because there will always be times when you don't have your gun on you. The sad reality is that our inalienable right is trampled upon at airports, government buildings, the entire state of Illinois and several other places. Starbucks says they're banned but who cares about that place with its sugar-filled milkshakes, skip that soulless franchise and support your local coffee shop. I'm sure it has more coffee and less ice.

Also, what are you going to do when you run out of ammo? If you haven't even been in a firefight, you'd be amazed how fast the ammo can be expended. No matter how many times you hit dead center on a paper target, the experience is simply different when there are lives on the line and the target is shooting back at you.

Martial arts are a great skill missing in the lives of many modern men. Here you can truly train yourself to become a warrior. It provides a brotherhood where you can exert your physical energy and meet other likeminded people. It is great for men and women alike. In my experience, these places tend to have people who are focused on maintaining a healthy lifestyle and live productive lives. If you can maintain an athletic physique, then you are at least capable of being disciplined in other areas of your life. Now, some in there will struggle to keep up with the physical exertion, but everyone is at different levels on their own Path to Manliness.

I remember when I first showed up to a Tae Kwon Do class. I did alright since I took classes as a kid, but I was rusty and a bit overweight. I have lost 25 pounds since joining earlier this year, this is in part due to changes in diet and regular trips to the gym, but Martial Arts are very helpful in getting your body back in fighting shape. After a few months, I am stronger, more flexible and better trained to defend myself no matter where I am. If you want to adopt the warrior mindset, this is the single most important way for you to do so.

Look in your gym or online and I'm sure your town will offer some form of martial arts. Find one with a knowledgeable instructor, check the reviews or attend a couple classes. Most places even let you do a free trial.

Also, if you have kids, this is the perfect way to teach them some self-defense skills and discipline. Martial Arts teaches proper form and technique in a fun but challenging manner that requires patience and dedication. The ranking system will motivate and reward your child for his or her efforts.

Learn to handle a firearm and legally carry one

Most people like to claim that they'll never need a gun because they don't live in a dangerous area. Yeah, I don't either. Yet I had to draw my gun once and almost had to a second time. Thankfully no one got hurt. You never know what type of situation you may be thrust into and it is always wise to be prepared.

What type of gun should you get? Get yourself a 9mm like a S&W M&P Shield or a Springfield XD. My first gun was a Springfield XDM in 9mm and though it looks big and intimidating, bigger guns handle the recoil better. 9mm is a perfect gun to start practicing with as the recoil is low, and the ammo is cheap. You could go get the much cheaper 22, but that has a tiny bullet that is not going to be effective in a firefight. Get yourself a 12-gauge shotgun by Mossberg or Remington for the home. Every self-reliant man (or woman) should have these two types of guns at a minimum.

If you go to a gun range, they'll help you learn how to shoot safely. Most of these places are happy to teach gun safety to newcomers and they always welcome new customers. If you have a friend who is into guns, ask him to take you to the range. Once you have your new shiny firearm, get licensed so that you can carry and protect yourself and your family.

Do your own research online as to the gun laws for your state or country. Look into everything from where and how to store your guns. Research what types of guns are legally allowed where you live and of course to what extent you are authorized to use force. These laws vary widely depending on your residence so do your own due diligence.

Keep yourself in peak physical condition

Now martial arts will help with this, but you'll want to spend some time in your local gym pumping iron too. There is simply no good argument for why a man should not be strong. A warrior is always prepared for the task at hand and being the strongest version of yourself is essential.

Personally, I hit the gym about 3 times a week and I do a solid 45 minutes of weights with a quick cardio warmup and cooldown. For cardio, I'll alternate between jogging, sprints, biking or rowing. Any of these are adequate for getting your heartrate up. When lifting, I rarely use machines as free weights will help strengthen your stabilizer muscles where machines will omit those muscles. Machines are generally better for isolation exercises, which have purpose too.

I bought this iron gym pull up bar for my home and it has helped me increase my strength. I used to struggle to do a pullup but can now hammer out several with great form. I even climbed a 15-foot rope for the first time in my life while preparing for Spartan Races. Though the rope climb is really about technique and abdominal strength, I now can climb a rope solely using my arms.

I also spend at least one day a week doing pure cardio. I find a trail or hit up downtown and go for a run. If you want a great spot, look for nearby college campuses. They tend to be set up to support pedestrian traffic and offer beautiful scenery. I'm talking about the green parks and old buildings you perverts! Plus, the youthful energy is always infectious and helps me hit peak performance.

Peak physical condition means eating right too. You need to stop eating processed junk and high carb diets. This will slow you down and make you struggle in the gym and on your runs. Since eating a more natural diet, I have seen my energy levels and performance spike; I tend to eat a high protein diet, lots of eggs and nuts, and a bunch of veggies. I also eat fruit. It is close to paleo, but not a 100% strict adherence to it. Moderation in all things.

Bottom line: If you are not already in athletic shape, that should be goal number 1 for you. Put down the potato chips and stop drinking so much beer. If you can't be disciplined enough to stay in shape, what makes you think that you will be disciplined in other areas of your life?

Adopt the warrior mindset and set out to conquer your life.

3. Push Through Your Limits

Paralysis by analysis is a huge problem for many young people today. They hold themselves back by self-imposed limits. The mindset of the warrior smashes through limits. But the typical person has no idea what they are truly capable of.

You likely have goals in your life, but you have no idea how small your goals are because you underestimate your true capability. Think bigger! Too many people are of the mindset that they can't ever write a book, or run a marathon, or guest star on a podcast. Quit setting limits on your capabilities, if you can conquer one thing that you view as impossible, your entire worldview will change.

These limits are self-imposed. Once you realize the truth, your world will bend to your will.

Remember the scene in the Matrix where Neo is waiting to see the Oracle? The little boy is bending spoons in the waiting room, he tells Neo that it is not the spoon that bends, but only yourself. Whoa....

I honestly don't think I ever understood this scene until I began to truly push myself past my own self-imposed limits. Early on in my self-improvement journey, I started saying what I couldn't do. I said I had limits, and now I'm crushing limit after limit. I have learned that I can't bend the spoon, but I can bend myself, and through bending myself, the world bends to my will. There is no spoon. There is no limit.

I couldn't run a 5K at the beginning of 2018. Later that year, I ran one in 31 minutes. I ran a second one in 22 minutes.

There is no spoon.

Last Spring, I ran a half marathon and I might run a full marathon in 2020.

There is no spoon.

I couldn't run a Spartan Race two years ago, yet I conquered it and in 2019, I completed my first trifecta, which involves running a 4-mile Sprint, 8-mile Super and a 13-mile Beast.

There is no spoon.

I wasn't built to climb a rope because of 'muh genetics' or whatever. I'm built big, now I can consistently climb a rope with relative ease, rain or shine.

There is no spoon.

Throughout 2018, I busted my ass all year. I lost 25 pounds, my goal was to lose 12 pounds by New Years - I doubled my goal and had time to spare.

What is the limit that you use to hold yourself back?

Is there a job or promotion that you keep talking yourself out of? Push yourself to new heights and go for it. Maybe you can't handle the pressure of the new job, but at least you'll learn something from the new experience. And who knows? You just might surprise yourself.

Or you could adopt the warrior's mindset and know that you will rise to the occasion and crush it. Most people do rise to the occasion, act now and see what new limits you can break. Remember: there is no spoon.

Is there a girl that you're too shy to talk to, because you lack confidence, possibly believing she's out of your league? Well, maybe it's time to brush off those tennis shoes and start running down local trails and getting yourself in shape. Maybe she doesn't want to date you, but she does want to date the man you can be 3 months from now: a better-looking man who takes care of his health.

If not her, then someone else. Maybe even someone better. Because once you feel confident in your skin and you get in shape, you'll find more women will be attracted to you and that abundance mentality will keep you from obsessing over that one girl.

Are you not a leader? You surely can be if you thrust yourself into a position where you are knowledgeable. Even with a little experience, a positive attitude and by carrying yourself with high energy, you can be a leader to other men, or kids. I've joined a leadership program in my community and it's amazing to see how many young people will look up to you and learn from you - I was the shy guy back in Middle School, but I broke through that self-imposed limit. There is no spoon.

We don't give ourselves enough credit. And we forget how lost we are in our youth. Young people love to see an older, positive role model. This is especially true if you are in good shape and provide wisdom, knowledge or a positive attitude; put all of these together and you can truly change lives.

Now, I love writing and seeing my readers follow in my footsteps and creating their own book and websites – so much so that it has inspired me to continue to spread this message. If you have stuck with this life-changing habit, you've likely found that it is easier to write 750 words on day 15 than it is on day 1. Lesson right there, gentlemen - if you can stick with your new habit, you will be amazed at the progress you can make in just a short amount of time.

Most people give up on new habits too quickly. Running is hard for many in the beginning, but as the weight begins to fall off and your lungs get stronger, you'll find that it begins to get easier - and dare I say, you may even begin to enjoy it. Now, I hate the treadmill, but I love getting outside and running trails or jogging around college campuses. There is no reason you can't do the same thing. You simply need to get started and in time, it can grow into a fun hobby.

Don't let your brain mindfuck you out of doing what you are fully capable of doing.

It is so easy to come up with excuses. One common trap is to buy into the lies that we tell ourselves, but this will only hold you back from reaching your full potential. Most people underappreciate the power of time. Maybe you can't do it today, but if you put in the time and effort, you'll be amazed what you can do next month. Imagine you stick with your new habit for a year, you can transform yourself into an entirely different person over the course of a year, and you have every reason to want what is best for you.

Those who achieve success in their lives are persistent in their daily habits. If you recognize the long-term benefits of pushing yourself a little bit each day, it's amazing how far you can go in 6 months to a year.

One thing to keep in mind is how will you feel when you run into people from your past? Most of us will see old faces for Christmas or Festivus or when we visit our hometown. How do you want your family to react to seeing you? How about old high school buddies or ex-girlfriends? Wouldn't it be great to run into that girl who dumped you and look positively stunning? This can serve as powerful motivation to push past your limits at the gym, running trails or getting up earlier to lead a more productive life.

4. You Need a Mantra to Motivate You

When I want to grab another plate of dinner or reach for that second, or third beer, I think to myself "Spartan Race" and it helps me fight off these base impulses. This subtle reminder that I have a Spartan Race coming up helps me maintain my discipline. The power of having a mantra in your head is magical; simple words can yield real world results.

A mantra is a powerful weapon because every single pound that I can lose will make it that much easier for me to carry myself through all these obstacles. This goes for normal everyday life as well; if you have fifteen extra pounds that you could lose, imagine how much easier your life would be if you could drop the weight – it's like carrying two gallons of milk with you all day long!

Words hold great power and so often we take them for granted. What we think, we say. What we say, we do. And we become what we do.

If you pay attention to your mood and energy while you are consumed with negative news on the mainstream media, you may notice that you are more irritable and angry. You may begin to wonder how what you consume in your life affects you. You'll really notice the difference if you stop watching these puppets on TV peddle fear to you and focus on a more positive life that centers on mindfulness, wellness and enjoyment. It is literally day and night. It can make you feel like a different person. Reborn. Resurrected like the phoenix out of the ashes. "Be the Phoenix!" There's a free one for you.

Keep this in mind when you look at the people you follow on social media. Every day I see people fall into this trap of outrage; it appears to be an addiction for many people to become a keyboard activist. I don't see very many happy or successful people doing this though. They waste their time resisting or gloating or whatever, but at the end of the day, it's an addiction. There are better ways to spend your time, and for some people, being this way is affecting their mental health.

There are also people who will complain about everything. Their behavior in real life mirrors their behavior online. These people are toxic and will sap you of your energy.

Every day you have so much mental energy to use - do not waste it. Too many waste their energy on fruitless worries, do not spread or entertain gossip. When those around you do so, ignore it. Gossiping is a waste of time and only small minds engage in this destructive habit. Great men rise above such pettiness.

You need to surround yourself with like-minded people and this becomes challenging as you begin to better yourself.

If you want a sense of belonging, drop the political nonsense, and join a tribe in your community. Join a karate class where you'll train together with like-minded people. Check out the classes being offered at your local gym. Instead of venting frustration and anger online, you can focus on your own self-development and connecting with others in your local community. This is how smart and motivated people manage their time; by channeling their energy in the most constructive manner possible.

All of this means nothing without action. If you want to see results, these words must come from the heart. This phrase must stir up all the adrenaline and fervor in your soul. These words should bring out the monster inside of you that you can unleash on the track or onto your squat rack. Kanye likes to talk about "Dragon Energy." Charlie Sheen would ramble about "Tiger blood." #Winning! There are many mediocre critics out there who love to poke fun at these sayings, but look at what the critics have accomplished compared to Kanye and Charlie Sheen?

There really is something to these slogans. It is always easy to criticize but when it gets results, then the critics are reduced to whiny spectators.

Stop judging and criticizing so that you can act to better your life. A rising tide raises all ships, so we should be positive and encouraging others to do the same. Critics see others succeeding as a reflection of their own shortcomings. That is why they want to tear you down. This crab in the bucket mentality is toxic. Ignore them. Focus on those that are positive and living out intentional lives.

Having a mantra is powerful, but only if it holds meaning for you. You need to be very clear with yourself about what it is that you want. You may say you want to be rich, but do you really? Have you given this any thought? It takes a lot of time and effort to make your dream a reality. It is only after you've begun to understand your true motivations that you can build the desire necessary to accomplish your goals. It is then that your everyday actions will work towards creating definite plans to acquire your desires.

Find your inner beast and change your life. What gets your blood pumping? What is your mantra? Share it with me in the comments below or tweet at me. People like to talk about building a personal brand, and all personal brands need a slogan. Your mantra is the slogan of your personal brand.

5. No More Zero Days!

Quit getting intimidated by the daunting tasks you set for yourself and start formulating and implementing incremental daily habits that sound easy.

Most people are obsessed with goals, because they're obsessed with results. These are the people who make goals every New Year's Eve and then start the new year with a hangover. Awesome start. Then these people are shocked when they lose motivation after a couple months and sink back into their old habits.

Then, there are people who obsess over habits and systems. Rather than obsess over the idea of being done, they enjoy the process.

Let's take writing for example. It's common to hear someone say they want to write a book, "someday." First off, "someday" is a vague word that offers your ego an out. By saying someday, you're giving in to the short-term temptation of doing something easier. You believe that you'll get to it later, but more often than not, "someday" never comes.

If you're truly interested in writing a book, you need to focus on the daily habits that will build over time to give rise to massive results. If you commit to write 500 words every single day, then you are committing to a process or a system that will get you closer to your goal every day. By writing 500 words a day, you are doing two things: One, you're getting a little better at writing each day. Two, you're developing a habit that will lead to a finished product.

The problem here is why you let zero days into your system. I'm pragmatic, even if you don't see me talk about my days off. You don't have to write every single day, but you should be writing nearly every day.

Don't Break the X!

Jerry Seinfeld has a famous system called "Don't Break the X" which he uses to write jokes every day. On a day he writes, he will mark an 'X' on his calendar and build up streaks. By visualizing his progress, his mind is motivated to work each day. After you've stacked a few days in a row, you won't want to "break the X." So, grab a physical calendar, place it somewhere that you'll see every day, and start your new habit. Don't break the X!

Who will be more likely to work out consistently? The guy who plans on running 10 miles or the guy who plans to simply put on his running shoes and show up. When you set out to accomplish a huge goal like running 10 miles, you're intimidated by the vastness of the goal from the very start. If you say you're simply going for a run, you trick your mind into thinking it's not a big deal. Half of life is simply showing up, because most people can't be bothered to even start.

When I sat down to write this book, I would get intimidated and freeze up if I thought about how massive this project was. So, I didn't think of it that way.

I broke it down into more manageable chunks. Each chapter is not too much bigger than a blog post, and I write one of those nearly every week – by sectioning my work, I find it less intimidating. I didn't start this project thinking; I'll write 35,000 words, I sat down and told myself "I want to write about these topics. I'll start with this one".

Use this system for all your intimidating goals. Every massive project you have can be broken down into smaller and more manageable tasks. You don't even have to be responsible for all these tasks, consider delegating some of your tasks to automation or other people.

If it's simple and unimportant, automate it. If it needs a more personal touch, hire someone to do it for you. If it is something that's important and difficult, you're likely going to be responsible, unless it's important but requires someone of a different skillset - then you'll be better served by contracting someone to do this for you.

There is a difference between a rest day and a zero day. Rest days serve a purpose. They are meant for your mind or body to recover from exerting tremendous effort. The problem is, too many people have zero days due to laziness or procrastination, not because they were rest days. And like most things, zero days tend to add up.

If you adopt the warrior's mindset, you'll realize that every day you get nothing done, is a day you give your enemies a chance to catch up with you. It won't happen overnight, but as these zero days stack up over time, you'll find that you lose momentum.

On the opposite side of the coin, if you consistently stack up little wins, you'll gain momentum. Life is all about habits.

What Creates Zero Days

Alcohol – You're out at the bars for a couple drinks and before you know it, your friend bought another round. "A couple drinks" becomes 6 or more. Suddenly you are out way later than you intended. You wake up late Saturday morning, hungover and tired from not sleeping well. Rather than getting in that workout or enjoying the beautiful morning, you lay on the couch watching Netflix or playing video games.

Video games – How many nights do you sit down to play a game and then another, and another. You get up to grab a late-night snack and realize it's 2 A.M. Your eyes are strained, and your mind is wired. How many weekends of your life do you want to devote to shooting at virtual pixels? Do you really get satisfaction from playing a warrior on a computer monitor? Video games give you a false sense of accomplishment. This is holding you back from achieving in real life by wasting your time and by mentally tricking your brain into believing that these are real life accomplishments.

Lack of Sleep – If you aren't fully rested, then you aren't going to be spending your time efficiently. Alcohol and video games are huge contributors to causing lack of sleep. Set limits for yourself so you don't go overboard. For both culprits. You may even have to give one or both up entirely. And stop staring at screens right before bed. Watch one less episode of Netflix and read a chapter in a book before you fall asleep. Keep your phone away from your room. If you really struggle to sleep, consider looking into CBD oil or magnesium. Magnesium deficiency is common in adults. Taking magnesium has been shown to help stabilize your mood and even relieve mild to moderate anxiety and depression.[14]

Sports – Everyone needs to relax a little and watching sports is a fun way to do so. This can be a great way to bond with your friends or kids. But too many guys let sports consume their lives by obsessing over every little stat and detail. For many, sports are a form of escapism allowing you to hide from real life problems. And I'm sorry but wearing another man's name on your back is a bizarre way of self-owning. You should be rooting for yourself.

Chasing girls – The typical young male mind is so obsessed with chasing girls that it essentially can become their hobby. You'll be researching how to talk to girls, how to meet girls and some even get into the philosophy of how to game girls just to get laid. This can become a tremendous waster of time and energy. There is a reason that I don't talk often about how to meet girls. It's because all the other information in this book indirectly increases your chances of attracting girls into your life. Become a higher value man, and you'll attract higher value women.

Stress – How many days have you let get away from you because you feel overwhelmed by everything on your plate? Get yourself a notebook and write down everything you need to get done. Then order these things in importance. And start at the top of your new priority list. Simply writing down everything that's weighing you down in your head is enough to lower your stress. And then as you knock off these tasks, you'll begin to feel lighter and a sense of real accomplishment.

6. Modern Life Needs a Rite of Passage

"Instinct trumps acquired knowledge when one's society is as corrupt as ours. The Spartan man grew wise in addition to his innate instincts, modern men grew fat and weak and liberal and their best instincts fell away like uterine fur. Ancient men grew better, into men. Modern men grew into mulch, compost, manure."

- *Roman McClay, Sanction*

Young Spartan boys were taken from their family between the age of 5 and 7 to live in an agele, Greek for pack, of other boys for their training. It was here they learned to compete with the other packs, instilling an appreciation for the tribal mentality at an early age.

Young boys are coddled in modern western civilization, especially those who are spoiled with the softness of affluence. And even those who make an average income can afford a very cushioned life. Who among your childhood friends struggled to survive in the elements or to find food? Never in the history of mankind has the average man lived such a soft life.

Spartan boys learn to read and write by age 10. Throughout their training they learn to become one with their weapon through dancing. Movement and footwork are essential to the Spartan warrior. As a part of their rite of passage into manhood, their hair was cut short, their tunics replaced with a cloak and they'd be thrown to the wild to test their merit.

Rather than testing the resilience and strength of young boys, we toss them into a feminized school where few male teachers are available to serve as positive male role models. And rather than to encourage the natural roughhousing that boys engage in innately, we drug them with amphetamines (Ritalin) and tell them to act more like girls.

In ancient Sparta, they encourage this natural behavior in boys and toughen them up by having them toughen their feet by walking barefoot. They were fed very little to keep them aggressive and hungry for more. This training was so intense and brutal that some Spartan boys would not survive.

In suburbia on the other hand, the young boy wants for nothing as he has a steady supply of high-sugar and highly processed junk food, endless entertainment and little to no struggle. Then, we as parents are shocked that our boys show no drive or enthusiasm to better themselves through hard work. Moral hazard allows them to be rewarded for laziness.

Their training was complete by age 20 and the Spartan boy would become a Spartan warrior. In ancient Greece, most cities were well known for their philosophy or culture. In ancient Sparta, they were known for their warriors who exemplified great character and resilience in battle.

"Sparta's walls are its men."

- *Lycurgus*

This is the Spartan Agoge. This is the Spartan Rite of Passage. This is what turns boys to men. Modern life needs a modern take on the Agoge.

I'm not clamoring for mothers and fathers to start shaving their kids' heads and throwing their young kids to the wolves in the forest. I am saying that if we expect to see our boys one day become men, that they will have to face hardship. For this is how we grow.

In modern culture, a boy becomes a man at 18 by passively waiting rather than being forced to show exemplary strength, honor or resilience through a rite of passage. In ancient cultures, a boy had to prove his worthiness to become a man. This is missing today, and it gives rise to the plethora of Peter Pan man-children who spend their days on Xbox, watching porn and binge drinking.

There is a serious problem with men today stuck in a prolonged adolescence. Many young men are postponing their lives under the guise of being responsible and "waiting for the right time". Comfortable lives encourage men to procrastinate everything from finding a serious career to starting a family.

The Agoge, meaning "education or upbringing," was designed to help boys transition into manhood. Teaching them to be resilient even through adversity that was quite literally life or death. To understand manners and etiquette to better fit in with the community, and to train for war, if the tribe needed defending from outside invaders.

These boys were also taught to speak with purpose, rather than to spout off nonsense to fill the void of quiet moments - an art that has been lost in recent years by a society that rewards only the loudest and most shocking. Spartan children learned the value of Laconism, or the act of speaking economically and with precision, the term came from the region of Laconia which was famous for its concise speaking.

Your Ego Conveys Confidence

Modern society wants you to be soft and to quieten down your ego. The dark truth is you should have an ego, you should believe in yourself, so long as you are competent enough to back it up.

The world has changed. While being humble may serve a purpose, you need to be able to sell yourself, your ideas and your mission. A man with no ego is a man who will never lead.

Donald Trump wasn't elected because of his humility. The average American voter sees his giant ego and assumes that in his great confidence, there is also competence. A man so proud of himself must be capable of great accomplishments.

Society wants you to think ego is a four-letter word. A modern-day leader of men must be comfortable with his ego, while keeping it in check. Life is all about balance.

Those who have lost control of their emotions are slaves to them. The same is true for those who allow their ego to grow too big for it to be controlled. Remember, balance.

So how do you draw the line between being overconfident and being confident? It is measured in competence. If you act like you're the best runner in the world, then you better be putting your fancy running shoes on the track and keeping up that image. If you say you're an entrepreneur and you shit on the 9 to 5 lifestyle, then you better have a solid financial base.

The real trick is when you push yourself a little too far so that you overreach. This is natural and happens to the best of us. Even Elon Musk couldn't hit the deadline for launching his Tesla Model 3. But Elon is a warrior and what does a warrior do? They go to war. By putting in 20-hour days and sleeping on the factory floors, he made it happen.

Ultimately, even if you have a massive ego, people love results. And if you slip up occasionally, they'll forgive you so long as you are close to the mark.

It is those who fear failure that never achieve greatness. By always playing the safe route, they protect their ego. But they don't allow it or themselves to grow. By accepting failure as a

natural part of the process, you can push
yourself to new limits.

7. The Seven Pillars of Masculinity

1. Be Authentic

In all forms of expression, be authentic. This means being true to oneself.

If you are going to work, you better be able to stand up for your ideas. If not, then you are a slave to your boss. If you are going to speak online, speak in such a manner that you would be comfortable having everyone from your mother to your priest reading your work. If you are going to act, then you better be able to defend your actions upon further scrutiny.

"To invent your own life's meaning is not easy... but it's still allowed... And I think you'll be happier for the trouble."

- *Bill Watterson*

What you think, you say. What you say, you do. What you do, defines your character.

Life is full of actors and imitators and people living inauthentic lives. You don't have to be a millionaire or a rock star to live a fulfilling life. To be fulfilled, you need to live a life that is authentic to your intentions and your principles.

When you live an authentic life, you are creating a life of freedom. Free from judgment, from living up to the standards of others, from fitting in with the tribe. By being true to yourself, you have liberated your mind, your actions and the very sense of your being.

Once you realize that this is an option, there is no going back.

"I used to always care what everyone else thought about me. Friends, coworkers, family, and worst of all: strangers. I was miserable. Getting over the fear of judgment was one of the best things to ever happen to me."

— Ed Latimore

It's normal to want to fit in with your friends and to live according to the expectations of your family. But it leads to anxiety and a life of fear. When you are constantly seeking to please others, you will find that you never make everyone happy, you, in turn can never be happy.

If you've read this though, you're not like everyone else. You have consciously sought to better yourself and to set yourself apart. So why are you still living like you're one of the average people in society?

If you listen to everyone's advice, don't be surprised if you end up like everyone else. They'll tell you to go to school and do what you're told and one day if you're lucky you'll be able to slave away making your boss rich.

To be rich is a state of mind. You may never reach a level where you have everything you want. Conversely, you can appreciate what you have. Live a life authentic to your own desires and you will find fulfillment.

2. Be Courageous

Vices are poison to the warrior monk. Be pure in mind, body and spirit.

It takes courage to live a life true to one's standards.

This may mean being brave enough to endure social pressure for standing up for your ideals. You need not be pressured into going out for drinks or wasting time in meaningless pursuits unless that is your intention. If you are so easily swayed, then you are not of free will.

Maybe you have a grand plan to start a new business. At the beginning there will be many doubters and critics who will tell you to take the easy road. The path of least resistance is seldom the road that leads to el Dorado. Once you achieve that success though, everyone will be lining up to get a slice of the pie - and yes, this will include many of those original doubters.

Being courageous means living a life true to one's own mission. While it may be easier to follow the well-worn path of working in corporate

America, is that a lifestyle that you can accept? There's nothing wrong with it, if you're happy with it. The problem is that many seek comfortable lives over fulfilling lives.

Be brave enough to pursue your own mission. Even if that means taking a more difficult path. An easy life and a better life are rarely synonymous.

It takes strength to be brave and this quality is inherent to the very definition of masculinity; the word conjures up images of men like The Rock or Jack Donovan, but it is not only strength in body.

A modern masculine man also must be strong of mind as well. Today's great men are warrior monks. The Knights Templar were described as warrior monks. Strive to be the modern-day equivalent by honing your spirit and your mind as well as your body.

Be vigilant, relentless and aggressive in the pursuit of your life's mission.

3. Have Honor

As the years go on, I watch society shed more dignity with each day. Obesity, sloth-like paces and general depravity are celebrated and accepted. What happened to self-respect, honor and discipline? Reclaim your manhood!

Get them in karate or MMA. This teaches honor, discipline and respect. Karate is one of the few places where you earn your way. Belts aren't given out without earning one first and it takes dedication to progress. The true sense of accomplishment is great for self-esteem.

Why bother training in a martial art when you can carry a gun? Because there will always be times when you don't have your gun on you. The sad fact of reality is that our inalienable right is trampled upon at airports, government buildings, the entire state of Illinois and several other places. I guess Starbucks says they're banned but who cares about that place with its sugar-filled milkshakes.

Also, what are you going to do when you run out of ammo? If you haven't been in a firefight, it is amazing how fast the ammo can be expended. No matter how many times you hit dead center on a paper target, the experience is simply different when there are lives on the line and the target is shooting back.

Martial arts are great skills missing in many lives of modern men. Here you can truly train yourself to become the warrior. They provide a brotherhood where they can exert their physical energy and meet other likeminded people; they are great for men and women alike.

These places tend to have people who are focused on maintaining a healthy lifestyle and living productive lives. If you can maintain an athletic physique, then you are at least capable of being disciplined in other areas of your life. Now, some in there will struggle but everyone is at different levels on their Path to Manliness.

I remember when I first showed up to class. I did alright since I took classes as a kid, but I was rusty and a bit overweight. I have lost nearly 25 pounds since joining in early 2018. This is in part due to changes in diet and regular trips to the gym, but Martial Arts are very helpful. After a few months, I am stronger, more flexible and better trained to defend myself no matter where I am. If you want to adopt the warrior mindset, this is the single most important way for you to do so.

Look in your gym or online and I'm sure your town will offer some form of martial arts. Find one with a knowledgeable instructor, check the reviews or attend a couple classes, most places even let you do a free trial for a couple classes.

If you have kids, this is the perfect way to teach them some self-defense skills and discipline. Martial Arts teach form and technique in a fun but challenging manner that requires patience and dedication. The ranking system will motivate and reward your child for his or her efforts.

4. Be Self-Reliant

Pride may come before the fall but leading a life of independence is truly gratifying. A man worth his salt is a man who first takes care of himself through hard work and creative pursuits. He then uses the fruits of his labors to benefit those around him; taking care of his family, his pets and his community.

One of the 9 noble virtues of the Vikings and the followers of Asatru is Self-Reliance.

Before you claim that I'm advocating for rape and pillage, understand that this cartoonish perception of Vikings has been crafted by Hollywood and the media at large. And sorry, Minnesota fans, but the Vikings didn't even have horns on their helmets - most of the Norse people were simple farmers.

There were Berserkers, warriors who, upon seeking out to conquer new lands, would amp themselves up for battle and charge the enemy fearlessly. This conjured up an image of invincibility in their enemies. A clever and fearsome battle tactic.

"Without enemies around us, we grow lazy. An enemy at our heels sharpens our wits, keeping us focused and alert. It is sometimes better, then, to use enemies as enemies rather than transforming them into friends or allies."

- Robert Greene

How can you be more self-reliant? Work hard to provide for yourself and your family. Set aside savings for a rainy day, this way you'll be prepared for life's curveballs. The Vikings were used to this mindset due to the harshness of the elements in Northern Europe with the long winters.

As an economist, I understand the power in division of labor, and I literally never change my oil, though I can change a tire. I can fell a tree and collect firewood if the power is out. I can cook a meal over a fire without electricity.

Life is full of adversity, and today's ideal man can thrive in these challenging situations. Many of us even enjoy the obstacle, it provides spice into our soft civilization.

The self-reliant man is complicated in a modern society that works cohesively to form a system that is mutually beneficial to all, even those who aren't independent. What matters is finding a positive way to contribute to society at large, and that can mean many more things than simply contributing financially. The effects of a man's time are often more valuable than a man's wealth.

5. Be Disciplined

"If you focus on the task at hand, shed all distractions, and follow reason with steadfast

determination, the divine spark within you will burst into flame."

- *Marcus Aurelius, The Meditations*

Be focused in all your pursuits and passions.

While most people crave freedom, they forget that discipline and freedom are two sides of the same coin. Without discipline, a life of pure freedom is anarchy. It is discipline that creates this life of freedom in the first place.

The problem with average people is they are fickle rather than disciplined; they seek quick riches and results. Average people don't want to put in the time and effort for the results they want.

If you want to be successful in life, it takes discipline. Simple things like exercising and eating right are too much for the average person, they'd rather make excuses than build a fulfilling life.

Waking up early on Saturday without a hangover is the mark of the enlightened man. He knows discipline and limits; he also knows the power in enjoying life as opposed to numbing himself with the products of corporate America.

If you're unsatisfied with your life, start planning a day in advance. Set a plan for tomorrow and stick with it, few are this disciplined.

6. Be Creative

My life really began to improve when I started writing. Why is this? Because life is much more fulfilling when you are creating more than you are consuming.

Don't be afraid to put yourself out there - be afraid of leaving this world wondering what if. I owe a lot of my positive results to a better lifestyle: reading more, writing more, exercising more, and most importantly, giving back: creating. Live a life of purpose.

The derivative of creation is consumption. What you consume will directly impact what you create. Read more books. This will make you more interesting and well informed. It also will help you become a better writer.

Never stop learning or sharing the knowledge you have amassed.

7. Mentoring the Youth

"So, in the majority of other things, we address circumstances not in accordance with the right assumptions, but mostly by following wretched habit. Since all that I've said is the case, the person in training must seek to rise above, so as to stop seeking out pleasure and steering away

from pain; to stop clinging to living and abhorring death; and in the case of property and money, to stop valuing receiving over giving."

– Musonius Rufus, Lectures

There are men who don't know who their father is, there are men who have been separated from their fathers, then, there are men who simply choose not to be involved in their child's life. This has created a void that I seek to help fill. And you can too.

Plenty are quick to condemn and lambast the younger generation. Few are willing to put forth their time and effort in helping this generation better themselves. I used to turn down opportunities due to a lack of confidence, now I'm part of leadership program in my community helping kids. Change your mindset. Change your world.

Society has attacked manliness in nearly all avenues of life, now we have a society filled with confused men who don't know what it means to be men. We have obliterated the nuclear family model and caused a generation to be raised without a positive male role model in the house.

The lack of positive male role models in the home, due to the family court system, in schools due to a lack of male teachers and elsewhere is leading to a young generation growing up with no sense of direction or purpose.

If you are angered by the perverse image of masculinity being portrayed by corporations, advertisers and the media, then it is your responsibility to take up the role of showing an accurate representation of positive masculinity.

Do this in your writing, in your speech, but most importantly, do this through your actions.

Men growing up without role models are at risk of ruining their lives. Out of all boys who become school shooters, 90% of the perpetrators are raised without a father.[16] These boys are also more likely to use drugs and become incarcerated. They also more frequently experience depression, have low self-esteem and perform poorly in school.[17]

You truly can make a difference simply by being a better role model.

Bonus: Persevere

Every day that you choose to persist,

Every day that you keep fighting -

That is you saying No to death.

Death is inevitable.

It is far too easy to give into nihilism, yet humanity doesn't. We keep fighting.

We get up and fight. We persist. Why?

Because you choose to

8. Every Day is a Battle

Successful people focus on long-term trends rather than the everyday ups and downs that get average people overly excited or demotivated. It's not about the extra couple pounds you pick up one week, it's about your monthly weight loss. It's not about making money every single day, it's about making money every month.

To prime yourself for battle, you better have the most optimistic outlook you have ever had in your life - your life depends on it.

This may not be a literal life or death battle, but the quality of your life depends on the little battles you face every day. You will likely win some battles, and lose others, but it's the overall war that truly matters.

When writing a book, you have a small battle every day. The obnoxious guru on Twitter, with a masculine name and fancy cars will tell you that he writes every day - the truth is, he likely tries to write every day, and comes very close but even he will lose the battle occasionally.

Some days he may forget to write, or he'll be too busy to get around to it. He might not feel like it one day. Then, there are days like the day I wrote this very chapter, where I simply opened the Word document and practically vomited out these 200 words with a near constant stream of conscious writing. It's more important to win the war than it is to win the battle.

The experienced writer knows that he needs to write every day, but he recognizes that not all days are created equal.

"The amateur waits for inspiration. The professional knows it will come after he starts"

- Steven Pressfield

So, why bother writing every day? Because it can be hard to tell which day is a good day. You need to give yourself the opportunity for success. If you only manage to tweak your chapter and add a few dozen words, that is still more than all those who never got out of bed. Remember: No Zero Days!

The first step is getting out of bed, the second step is making your bed (if you are a devout follower of Saint Jordan B. Peterson... And in his holy name... amen!) Sincerely though, if you don't have a reason to get out of bed, then how can you expect to do anything meaningful in this life?

I talk about this very situation repeatedly in my first book, Reclaim Your Manhood. You need to have a life mission: this will be your reason to get out of bed. There will be days where you won't want to get up, and put in the work, which is normal! Having a mission will inspire you to push yourself on the days where you aren't feeling it.

We are going to take that idea a step further in this book.

NOW I NEED YOU TO BELIEVE IN YOUR MISSION!!!

Words like doubt, disbelief, can't or won't, are energy vampires that destroy your mission. Wipe them out of your lexicon! Replace them with positive words and your actions will follow suit.

Act as if you are already at the end of your mission and you are the expert in your field. If you want people to believe in you, then you better believe in yourself first.

This may sound like some new age bullshit but there is a reason why this works.

1. It conveys confidence
2. It creates a positive mindset
3. It focuses you on a goal

The average person wants to be led, and they are looking for a man who is confident; it signals expertise and heuristically we are drawn to believe the signal. Whether true or not, we simply don't have time to do everything and we are forced to outsource many tasks in our daily life.

Grab a pen and a piece of paper. Draw a line while staring at the ending point of your line. Now do the same while staring precisely where your pen lays. Which line looks straighter?

The first line. This metaphor signifies how if one is to achieve success in their current course, then one must focus on where they are going. This may seem obvious yet so many will focus on how things can go wrong or worry over past events. If you want to achieve success, focus on what you need to do to make it happen, focus on your destination to stay on the right path.

An end point is your motivation. When you see the lifestyle and the results you are working towards, this will inspire you to work harder. On the days when you aren't quite feeling it, this will serve as a reminder to keep pushing.

Look at the most successful people in the world and you'll see they have an optimism that can't be shaken by the failures they surely faced. If you are like me, you are blown away by Elon Musk launching a Tesla into space and past Mars. What most people forget to notice is the dozens of rockets that blew up on the launch pad before he finally got it right.

Failure is merely a pitstop on the road to success.

The Pen is the Sword at Scale

"It is said the warrior's way is the twofold way of pen and sword, and he should have a taste for both ways."

– Miyamoto Musashi

This quote is from The Book of Five Rings. A powerful book written by an ancient Japanese warrior who mastered the art of sword dueling, besting over 60 opponents by the sword. If you appreciate The Art of War by Sun Tzu, you'll love this book; it is written in a similar style and offers timeless life lessons that are applicable in battle and in daily life.

This quote struck me as particularly profound, and it received a lot of engagement on Twitter when I posted it. I was reminded of the Knights Templar who described themselves as Warrior Monks. I love this term for its balanced approach and have sought to emulate this lifestyle in my daily battles. Anyone who pursues excellence should adopt this balanced approach because daily life is a battle. My question to you is, how many of these battles do you win?

Every day is a battle. Every day there is a winner. Every day there is a loser.

I'm pragmatic and recognize that it is unreasonable to win every battle, but a Warrior Monk should cultivate the mindset that every day you have the potential to win said battle. Every time you lose a battle, you must see it as a teaching moment and learn to better yourself for the next battle. Adopt the warrior's mindset and set yourself up for success! How do you do this?

The Way of the Pen

Every night, get your pen and notebook out and craft your battle plan. Write down a list of goals. What do you need to do to accomplish these goals? Start writing out your daily tasks and prepare your mind to accomplish these tomorrow. Cross off each task when finished for a sweet hit of dopamine. Fuck yeah.

Anything you don't accomplish gets added to the next day's list. I aim to complete three significant tasks every day; in addition to my regular routine. These tasks are more focused towards a goal that I'm working on - typically, along the lines of cold outreach to new clients or working on a project like this book.

Like anything else, this habit can be difficult to start but over time becomes second nature.

A Warrior Monk wakes up ready to conquer each day. While not necessary, I recommend getting up early as this sets the tone for your day. This allows you to accomplish so many tasks before the average person takes a shower, hot or cold. I have also found that not all hours of the day are created equally; morning hours tend to be productive, focused on writing, reading, working out or meditation. Night hours tend to focus more on hedonism or sloth: Netflix, alcohol or video games.

*These results are based on the life habits of Ryan Felman. Your results may vary. Past events are not indicative of future occurrences. If you find yourself with an erection lasting longer than four hours, please consult your physician. Terms and conditions may apply. Not valid in Hawaii or Alaska.

Order of Assassins

"They call him Shaykh-al-Hashishim. He is their Elder, and upon his command all of the men of the mountain come out or go in ... they are believers of the word of their elder and everyone everywhere fears them, because they even kill kings."

- *Benjamin of Tudela*

The Order of Assassins or Assassins are an Islamic sect from the 11th century.[3] They were led by a man named Hassan-I Sabbah, who inspired the Assassin's Creed video game series, it was he who originally said, "Nothing is true, all is permitted."

Their group was called the Assassins, but most did not engage in combat. Those who did were known as the fida'I, translating to "self-sacrificing agents."[4] They resorted to assassinations out of necessity due to lack of an army, they were responsible for the assassinations of two caliphs, many sultans and several Crusader leaders.[6]

The Crusaders feared the Assassins in part due to the embellishment of their stories by Marco Polo. The Assassins were known for eliminating prominent targets in front of an audience to intimidate their enemies, this led to their legendary reputation that still exists to this day.

The origins of this secretive order are elusive and mysterious. In 1256, the Mongols destroyed their headquarters, Alamut, in modern day Iran. Much of the information of their origins were written by enemies or based on legends. The Holy Land was a place of great violence at the time due to the Crusades. Hassan-I Sabbah was said to have formed the order to exact vengeance on his enemies.

Marco Polo tells of a man whose followers were so loyal, possibly due to being drugged by hashish and promised to be led to "paradise."[5] According to Marco Polo, upon being drugged, the fida'I would be taken to a "secret garden of paradise." The assassins would awaken in this garden and find themselves surrounded by beautiful young maidens and beautiful plants, an old man would explain that they are witnessing their place in Paradise and that if they served the Order's cause, they would find eternal pleasure.[7]

These Assassins were patient and calculating in their attacks. They were trained to blend in with the surroundings of their targets and possessed great knowledge of their enemies, and the culture and language of their enemies.

These assassinations were typically meant to reduce violence against their order. They waged vengeance against those who had committed massacres against the Assassins' order.

The Assassins were well trained in the Islamic warrior code, Furusiyya. They trained in combat, disguises, linguistics and the art of war.

They were known for employing psychological warfare against their enemies in favor of overt warfare. During the Seljuk invasion, a Seljuk Sultan named Sanjar refused peace negotiations offered by the Assassins. One morning, the Sultan awoke in bed and when he opened his eyes, he found a dagger stuck in the floor near his bed.

Later a messenger from the Assassin's order stated, "Did I not wish the sultan well that the dagger which was struck in the hard ground would have been planted on your soft breast." This resulted in a ceasefire for several decades.[2]

The downfall of the Assassin's Order came at the hands of the Mongol Empire who besieged Alamut on December 15, 1256, which was retaken by the Assassins for a few months in 1275 only to be defeated once again. Though many of the Assassins committed Taqq'iya, which is the act of hiding their true identities, waiting for their Imams to revive the order.

The Way of the Sword

Prepare your body for daily combat - whatever that means for you. I recommend lifting weights and cardio. I see marathon runners with times that are significantly faster than mine, but if caught in a tight space, I'd make short work of them in hand to hand combat. I also see bodybuilders who couldn't outrun an old lady in a motorized scooter because they are so heavy. Seek balance in your physical pursuits.

I lift weights about 3 times a week. This gives me strength of body and solace in mind. Without an outlet for physical aggression, I would struggle to maintain serenity throughout my day. This is what helps me remain a civilized member of society rather than a bloodthirsty barbarian wearing the hide of a wolf and living in a makeshift hut down by the river with a fellow band of brothers. Though there are days where I question my decision here.

Your body needs to be active! I run once or twice a week, usually about 5K, though I'll push myself occasionally. Lately my runs have been exceeding 10 miles and I recently ran a half-marathon. In January of 2018, I struggled to breathe after running a single mile; today I can run 10 without too much trouble. With practice and dedication, the modern warrior can become formidable in any pursuit he chooses.

Running has become a beautiful moment of active meditation for me. An oxymoron - perhaps, but my mind wanders, and while running I find peace of mind and often many of my most profound thoughts. This is especially true as you creep into those longer distances; the mind stills and you can really delve deep into those subconscious thoughts that are floating around in there. In a world full of constant noise, seeking quiet is a rebellious and worthy endeavor.

You'll also gain a newfound perspective for your city when you hit the pavement. It's a more intimate look into the place that you call home. By getting out of your car and slowing down a bit, you can really appreciate your surroundings; this allows you to practice awareness, which allows you to notice the little details that paint a picture.

Practice being present and see what you notice.

I highly recommend training in martial arts; not only to learn self-defense but to gain a community of like-minded individuals who want to push themselves. Through persistent training, devotion and a proper mindset, martial arts train one to be aware of your surroundings. It teaches one that persistent action over time creates powerful results. It provides you with a group of strong-willed individuals that will help keep you accountable in your life mission.

I have taken Tae Kwon Do and Jiu Jitsu classes for about two years now. When I first showed up, I was soft, out of practice and overweight. Now that I swapped my drinking buddies for motivated and athletic friends, I've lost over 30 pounds, learned new self-defense skills and gained a team that I can run obstacle course races with. The people you spend time with have a profound impact on your life. Do not underestimate.

In my academy, I've witnessed people get out of shape, and they get called out on it. The amazing thing is rather than make excuses, they lose the weight and get back on the right path. The modern world is filled with safe spaces and judgement free zones. If you long to return to a world of sanity and boundaries, then martial arts are for you.

Too many are concerned with being politically correct and not hurting anyone's feelings. Being politically correct will do you no favors in a street fight. Martial arts retain the harshness of a world that believes in truth and accountability. This is to the betterment of all involved.

What few people realize is how mental physical activity can be. The gym is my church and I regularly worship at the house of iron. Without these activities, I wouldn't simply lose my physical prowess but also my mind. I gain my mentality through physicality. By pushing myself and making myself stronger, I gain the confidence to win my daily battles consistently and ruthlessly. If you want to crush this year, you must start by winning your daily battles.

The average person today feels lost, because they don't make time for introspection or reflection. They drift from distraction to distraction. They dull their senses with drugs and alcohol. These people are miserable, and they don't even take a few minutes each day to meditate on the state of their affairs. These people are sleepwalking through life.

Life without introspection is a life of slavery - slavery to our base impulses and shallow desires. Discipline is our liberator from this bondage. By staying consistent to our pursuits, we can be free to be who we want to be.

"I must create a system or become part of some other man's."

- *William Blake*

Throughout the day, the average person will find themselves adrift without purpose.

This is why I build systems to work towards building my own path, to work on my projects and to build my brand. You'll find that with purpose, it is much easier to find motivation and it will last longer.

Through the implementation of these systems, I can maintain progress towards my goals. In the inevitable event that I get stuck or lost, I merely resort to my list of daily routines (more on that in Chapter 11: Craft the Ultimate Routine) and regain my focus.

This is how you craft a life of freedom for yourself. You build yourself a system. You build your daily routines. In these flashes of momentary confusion, you have the perfect system to realign your mindset, to stay on the right course and to continually better yourself. This is how the most successful people manage to remain so consistent in their endeavors.

"There are but two powers in the world, The Sword and The Mind. In the long run The Sword is always beaten by The Mind."

- *Napoleon Bonaparte*

9. Introspection is the Path to True Self

A wise man sees the value of making time for introspection.

"Very little is needed to make a happy life; it is all within yourself, in your way of thinking."

    - Marcus Aurelius

Thoughts are profound, but writing will have a longer lasting impact. What is particularly interesting is when you look back at your writing from 6 months or a year ago, you'll realize the extent of the progress you've made. This gives you a glimpse into your own mindset from a different time and lends perspective on how you've grown as an individual.

I am typing this out onto my laptop, and you are reading thoughts that I had from back in 2019. This provides an interesting perspective when reread later by offering a glimpse into a different period in one's life. Essentially, it is a form of time travel.

The power of reading books is a form of connecting with minds of the past. This is an especially powerful concept when one is reading books written by influential minds in ancient times. For example, nearly every day I read from The Meditations by Marcus Aurelius, and every day I am transported into the mindset of Rome's greatest general who lived nearly 2,000 years ago. What is amazing is how relevant and relatable many of his problems are today.

A simpler and more hands-off approach, though perhaps more challenging - is to meditate. Meditation has become a bit of a meme for people who want to sound spiritual or flex that they're working on their own self-improvement.

Normal people (that's polite for mediocre) like to scoff at the idea. These are the same people who will simultaneously claim to wish for a fit body and attractive physique while shoveling mass quantities of alcohol and processed food in their mouth at breakneck speed. To witness the wild beast in action, one need only stalk the herds as they graze the buffet lines at the local Golden Corral.

Most people spend so much of their life poisoning themselves with a steady stream of alcohol and processed food, that this becomes their normative state. They simply accept feeling lethargic all the time. All it takes is a few weeks of eating natural food and you'll see what you've been missing out on all these years.

Meditation can show you a whole new outlook on life, if only you let it. Aristotle says, *"It is the mark of an educated mind to be able to entertain a thought without accepting it."* You simply need to drop your ego and open your mind. This is the method for communicating with the Universe, for the Universe is mental.

Keep an open mind and entertain new ideas. The universe is always changing. The world is always changing. You are always changing.

Look through past journal entries and you will see change. Here you will find evidence of personal growth. These changes can be subtle and insignificant when peered at from day to day, but when you look over a journal entry from 6 months ago, these changes suddenly seem drastic. You may barely even recognize the person you once were.

Many of these thoughts you have are half formed or premature. By capturing them in your journal, you are giving your future self to come back to them with a new perspective. Ideas that confused you at the time of writing may become life changing revelations upon a second look.

If you simply let these thoughts leave your mind as easily as they enter, you may miss out on these priceless lessons. Capture them. Organize them. Meditate on them.

Introspection is the Path to Self-Discovery

Writing down your thoughts is tantamount to having an intimate discussion with yourself. Find yourself a quiet and uncluttered spot to delve into the depths of insanity and see what value comes forth.

You need not be ashamed of your own thoughts. Society likes to organize people into neat little boxes so that we can be more easily managed. The truth of our nature is we are all a little crazy in our own ways and this is what gives humanity its beauty. Let your freak flag fly and show your authentic self. There is nothing more boring than people playing it safe all the time for fear of judgment of others. When you learn to be honest with your wants and feelings, you achieve a true sense of self and through this, and you may finally cultivate a life of purpose.

The man who constantly fears society's judgment is forever a slave. The man who is comfortable expressing his own crazy self is a free man.

Life without introspection is a life of slavery. Slavery to our base impulses and shallow desires. Discipline is our liberator in this bondage. By staying consistent to our pursuits, we can be free to be who we want to be. It is the discipline to stay true to our long reaching goals that allows us to actualize our true self and grow as a person. Anyone can act on a whim and say they are free, but are they truly content and fulfilled?

Most likely the same people who claim to want to write a book or start a company are not disciplined enough to focus on such long-term aspirations. The world has grown so accessible that the temptation to fulfill short term pleasure is constantly available and easily within reach. It is simply easier to push the Netflix button on the remote, than to search within and find the wisdom inside that could, over time, develop into a book.

So, although accomplishing your goals have become more achievable than ever, the amount of distractions in your path has never been higher. There will always be an infinite amount of content to consume, keeping you distracted from your mission; but if you can stay focused, there are more tools available to you than ever before. With the internet, everything is faster.

The modern world rewards people who can postpone pleasure and pursue these greater, long-term aspirations. The choice is yours. You can live with no respect or acknowledgement of your future and one day wonder how you got to this point. Or you can do some soul searching and find your true desires and pursue your goals. Don't be mediocre. Be awesome!

10. Daily Habits to Stay on the Right Path

"All of humanity's problems stem from man's inability to sit quietly in a room alone."

- *Blaise Pascal*

Meditation

"The happiness of your life depends upon the quality of your thoughts."

- *Marcus Aurelius*

Spend 5 minutes of your day in silent solitude and you will find peace and clarity. Maybe it's not that simple, but will help you reduce stress. If you need guidance on how to start this, try the free app, Insight Timer.

This app has guided meditations that can give you an idea of how to get started. I found them helpful in the beginning but now I meditate in silence. The app is good for this and it has a timer, as the name implies. It also tracks your stats and this gamification of the process can inspire you to keep up the practice.

Many people ask me about getting rid of bad habits. One of the most effective methods for quitting bad habits, is to replace them with positive habits.

Meditation is an example of a positive habit you can use to replace an old bad one. Most people are so wrapped up in the chaos of daily life that they never take a moment to simply breathe. It is an act of rebellion to seek peace and silence in a time when there is so much noise and stimulus.

When I practice meditation, I will take a seat looking outside through my window. I close my eyes, but I still sense the positive energy of nature, this helps me to meditate. I use this app to set a time limit - 5 to 10 minutes. While meditating I will sit still, close my eyes and focus on my breath. I breathe slowly and thoughtfully using deep breaths.

Rather than to worry about my mind wandering from place to thought to randomness, I accept each thought. I ponder it, and occasionally focus on this thought for the duration of my meditation. Other days, I'll remove the thought quickly and return to silence.

Each day's meditation is different, and each day will offer different pieces of wisdom or epiphanies. Though it may not always feel productive, the practice and habit itself are important to achieving a more mindful lifestyle.

Meditation, like nearly anything else, can be improved with practice. At first, it will feel awkward. Let go of these thoughts of self-consciousnesses. In time it will be as natural as breathing. See what I did there?

Meditation can induce relaxation. It has been said to help fight disease. "The more people practiced relaxation methods such as meditation or deep breathing, the greater their chances of remaining free of arthritis and joint pain with stronger immunity, healthier hormone levels, and lower blood pressure."[11] It helps balance emotions and can promote tranquility. A meditation practitioner does not hold onto negative emotions for as long as people who do not practice mediation.

I now meditate every day and see numerous benefits in my life from the practice. Seek the silence.

"Buddhists believe the reality we live in is not the ultimate one. There's another reality we can tap into that's unaffected by our emotions, by our everyday world."

- *Dr. Herbert Benson*

Journaling

"What ailment of yours have you cured today? What failing have you resisted? Where can you show improvement?"

- *Sextius*

This quote by Sextius is worth contemplation, and journaling.

People often ask me, "What I should journal about?" This ancient quote offers endless opportunity for writing, and if you turn this into a daily practice, you'll see great improvements in the quality of your life.

If you can't come up with interesting content to write about, there are two big solutions to this common problem.

First, start doing more interesting things. Many people who say they have nothing to write about spend most of their time watching Netflix, playing video games or drinking at the bar. These hobbies are so commonplace that no one will be interested in the stories derived thereof.

Have the courage to step out of your comfort zone and take on new hobbies. Take that class on pilot's lessons, take up a martial arts class, buy a kayak. The real world is infinitely more interesting than the matrix of Netflix and video games. Once you realize this, it becomes intoxicating - a positive addiction.

Secondly, read more books. If you spend most of your time watching sports and television, you'll have fewer interesting topics to delve into. Conversely, if you focus on interesting non-fiction books, you will constantly be learning new material to dissect.

Reading books gives you a massive advantage over the army of average people who'd rather spend their time watching sports or binging on Netflix. The fast-paced nature of social media has made focus on deep work a habit that is increasingly rare. Taking the time to ignore your phone and delve into a book is to gain wisdom and insight into the world, and there are no limits to the advantages you can gain from the massive library available to you.

Read. Meditate on what you read. Write about it and if it is worthy, share it with the world.

Exercise

How you start your day speaks volumes on your priorities. Nearly every single one of my days begins with writing or exercise - usually both. This really sets the tone for the day.

The modern man has become fat and lazy. He is addicted to gaming and mindless consumption, he worships doctors, while ignoring his nutrition and exercise, he loves thots online but fears social interaction in the real world. Reclaim your manhood!

If you want to be successful in life, it takes discipline. Simple things like exercising and eating right are too much for the average person; they'd rather make excuses than build a fulfilling life.

One of the most effective ways to motivate yourself to run is to set a deadline. If you're not a runner, go online and find a 5K race. Sign up and pay for it - now you're committed. Then go out and train; every week, you'll have this race motivating you to train.

In 2018, I realized I had never run a 5K in my life. I told myself that I was "not a runner." So, I found a race nearby and signed up for it. I was about 30 pounds heavier at the time, but I wanted to see how I would perform. To my surprise I finished with a time of 32 minutes. Not too bad for a first race.

And I know what you're thinking: "The only way I'd run that far is if someone is chasing me."

I've heard this about 100 times in the past year. Most people hate running. They say it's unnatural, they say mankind wasn't meant to run. This is an outright lie to defend your lack of motivation to run.

Ancient men didn't hunt animals with Remington 700 bolt action .308 rifles. Ancient men didn't run down a gazelle and bite their neck from behind. Ancient men didn't jump out of a bush and snatch a bird from the air. So how did we eat meat?

We ran. We ran like a flock of seagulls. We simply out endured our prey because we can sweat, and we can breathe while running - even a lion must stop to catch its breath, but humans were made for long distance running.

As insane as it sounds, mankind was made for running long distance, it's natural and it will make you feel connected to your ancestral past, your mind will wonder, thoughts emerge, endorphins flood your system and you'll feel happy and proud of yourself. You'll feel worthy. You'll feel strong.

It's not that you're "not a runner." It's that you are out of sync with your ancestral roots. You've forgotten who you are.

Practice

It is important for a warrior to keep his skills sharp. The modern warrior who doesn't practice consistently will find his skill dulling over time.

This is all too common, especially when you begin to experience a degree of success. The spoils of success make you weak. When you grow up with nothing, it takes little discipline to eat right. Your hunger lies in your mission, not the kitchen. But as your bank account grows, you grow satiated, this leads to you abandoning your mission.

With more success comes more comfort. Most of us forget that it is all our disadvantages, our struggles, the adversity that we overcome that shape us into becoming stronger. The strongest swords are forged in fire.

This is really the secret to life. Practice makes perfect and its affects take time to see. Most people simply give up too quickly. You convince yourself that those who have achieved success did so because they had an unfair advantage, you claim they have something that you don't. This is your ego defending yourself, you're making excuses because you don't want to put in the work.

The truth is that there's really nothing unique about those who succeed. They simply work harder and put in the time. So, while people will claim that they were dealt a bad hand, most of these people never bother to play. They simply fold their hand with each deal, sit at home and mope, and spend most of their time living in the matrix of video games, porn, mindless scrolling and Netflix.

Imagine what might happen if you took the real Red Pill. The truth that you can better yourself.

This is how you shape your own reality. Want to become a stronger man? Hit the weights consistently. Want to become a writer? Start writing every day. Want to get more comfortable talking to girls? Approach girls consistently.

It's when you stop doing these things that your skills become atrophied.

Seneca: "He who studies with a philosopher should take away with him some one good thing every day: he should daily return home a sounder man, or on the way to become sounder.

11. Craft the Ultimate Routine to Conquer Each Day

"You will never change your life until you change something you do daily. The secret of your success is found in your daily routine."

-   *Jon C. Maxwell*

You need to stack small wins to build up momentum. Too often you will waste time struggling to figure out how to start. You need to standardize your daily process to be more efficient with your time. So how do you do this?

You need a routine. Why? Because some days you're tired, or groggy or you don't feel well. By sticking with a ritualistic routine, you will maintain your mission through good and bad days. So, what makes a good routine?

First, you need to wake up early. I wake up around 5 or 6 in the morning almost every day. Why? Because not all hours of the day are created equal. Morning hours are significantly more productive than night hours. Night hours are for Netflix and gaming. Morning hours are for your mission.

The modern-day warrior knows how to exercise self-control. He is the master of his impulses and is immune to binge watching TV at night. This is a massive advantage; this allows him to get to sleep early so that he can wake up refreshed and ready to declare war on the new day.

Drink water first thing in the morning. You want to drink roughly 64 ounces a day to stay healthy and hydrated, so start by knocking out 8 ounces right away - this also will help you stave off hunger. The sensation for thirst and hunger are very similar and drinking water instead of snacking will help to maintain your warrior physique.

This is the easiest lifehack you will ever hear. Just drink water. Keep a bottle of water near your bed so it's literally as easy as possible to do. Reach for your water bottle first thing; not your phone.

Body

Every morning, I play an upbeat song, I roll out of bed and do some light stretching as I prepare to start my day. I hop on the exercise bike and start warming up while watching Joe Rogan for inspiration and entertainment. Due to his expansive list of informative and motivated guests, I learn amazing wisdom with every episode. Good information into your brain produces good information coming out.

Podcasts are a much better input than the news. You think you need to be better informed by the news, but has it really benefitted your life?

Instead, by listening to the Joe Rogan Experience, I've learned all sorts of health tips, fitness techniques and have had plenty of laughs as well.

I try to stay away from pills, alcohol and caffeine. I have never found coffee to be that effective at waking me up so much as making me a junkie that depends on it for my next fix. So, I opt to exercise early in the morning to get the creative juices flowing. 25 pushups do more for you than a cup of coffee, and you'll look better for this healthy habit.

Even if you only devote a few minutes to the exercise bike, getting your heart rate up is perfect for shaking off the morning grogginess. Not only that, but because I enjoy watching Joe Rogan interviews, I'm motivated to get out of bed without ever hitting snooze.

This is the secret to avoiding the snooze button. When you go to bed at night, think about 2 or 3 things that you're excited to do tomorrow. If you're motivated enough to wake up early and workout, this could be your motivation. If you have a podcast you want to listen to, this could be your reason for getting out of bed. Find a reason to get up and moving.

There is no reason to start your day doing something you hate. Too many people go to bed late, hit snooze and then wake up agitated and anxious as they rush to get ready for work. This is not how mankind was meant to live.

Exercise every day. You need to be active. Every day you need to train to be harder to kill. This will affect your mood and your self-esteem. Chemically, the endorphin boost you get from working out will make you happier. The effects it has on your body will make you feel better about yourself, more energized, more confident. Your options are endless: running, lifting, biking, hiking, martial arts... The world is your playground.

Mind

No one reads anymore. If you can consistently read and learn from books, you will become a real-life superhero. Reading books allows you to connect on an intellectual level with the greatest minds in history and the most successful people of the modern era. There is a wealth of information out there that will help you live your best life.

"It is chiefly through books that we enjoy intercourse with superior minds. In the best books, great men talk to us, give us their most precious thoughts and pour their souls into ours."

- *William Ellery Channing*

Intelligence can be gained through willpower. By simply reading three books on a subject, you'll be better versed than most of the population. The trick is to start being more mindful about the way you read. Turn your phone off and set it in another room to allow yourself to fully engage with your book. While reading, I highly recommend highlighting important parts and taking notes.

You need to rethink the way you read. While most people view reading as merely a box to check off, there can be so much more to gain from it. If you take your time and enjoy the book and fully process it, you can take much more and add it to your life. Take notes on what is important. Meditate on interesting ideas. If you're a writer, these ideas can inspire you to writer about new ideas.

Practice being in the moment and fully engross yourself in what you are reading. Meditate on what you read. How can this affect your life? Do you agree with what's being said? If you disagree, then why? Do you really disagree or did the content simply make you uncomfortable by reevaluating your own life choices? What can you add to the topics brought forth and can you share them with your friends, family or followers?

Read inspirational emails to get a glimpse into the mind of motivated individuals. There are amazing people with blogs or Twitter accounts pumping out free content on a daily basis. If you take the time to learn from them, it is amazing what you can accomplish. Every day I read emails from many of these dedicated and self-motivated people. They help inspire and educate me in numerous ways by sharing their daily habits, problems and solutions.

These content creators keep me in the right mindset and help to hold me accountable. They educate me with the wisdom and ideas they have discovered. They input positive energy into my brain, which helps me put forth positive energy back into the world.

All this consumption is meaningless if you don't find a way to give back. I am constantly advocate creative writing - everyone should be writing, even if you're not a writer. You'll never learn more about yourself than when you start writing.

"My life really began to improve when I started writing."

-   *Ryan Felman*

What if you're not good at writing? That's ok. I can help. My most effective tip is to never start with a blank page. One foolproof method to avoid the dreaded blank page is to write about a quote that inspired you. How does that quote impact your life on a personal level? Does it inspire you? Challenge you? Anger you? Once you start writing, the words flow much more smoothly.

So many people get hung up on that opening line or paragraph. Don't worry about making it perfect on your initial draft. Simply get your basic ideas down, you can come back to it later and refine it. That opening line is often easier to writer after you've finished your first draft.

Write about what you did today and how it affected your day. Write about your ideal life (My first ever blog post). Get started today and you'll improve tomorrow. In time, writing will feel more natural and instead of struggling to find the words, you'll struggle to find the time to write all you have inside your head.

What really separates the professionals from the amateurs is that the pros will write every day, even when they don't feel struck by the mood. Amateurs wait for inspiration. Professionals will stick to their system and make it happen, no matter how painful.

One of the most underutilized tools to the modern writer is social media. While most people will use it to engage in mindless scrolling, those who recognize its potential wield it to their advantage. As you are writing, you'll constantly find yourself second guessing lines, paragraphs and well, nearly all of it some degree.

Social media can be the perfect tool to receive instant feedback on your writing. Post that line that you're unsure of and look to see how your followers respond. Either you'll have the confidence to leave it as is, or you'll get free critical feedback helping you tweak the weaker spots of your writing.

One of the biggest weaknesses in modern life is the lack of social cohesion. You should be reaching out to people nearly every day - it's called social media for a reason. We are social people. Every day, I will reply to people's mass emails, their blog posts or tweets that resonate with me. I do this without expectation of reciprocity. I simply offer gratitude or my thoughts on the matter at hand. This may make their day, or get you on their radar. You never know how one small act could lead to massive results in time.

You should be networking every day: message people, email people, call people. Reach out and forge meaningful relationships. Most people are unwilling to even attempt this. This is life-changing advice. Act on it.

Spirit

Modern life is sedentary for most of us, but by nature, we are not sedentary creatures. Find a way to introduce activity into your daily life and watch your spirit and mood elevate. Martial Arts academies and gyms are excellent places to meet like-minded people. Train to be harder to kill. Find a hobby and you'll find people who share your interest.

My favorite day of the week is Monday because I enjoy a fresh start, but also because of the Martial Arts training I do. While most people hate Mondays, it holds a special place in my heart. This is because after class, I attend another hour-long class where my classmates and I focus on more intense training to prepare for running Spartan races. Few things in life are better than training with like-minded people in intense physical and mental challenges. This is how brotherhoods are formed.

Do you remember what Tyler Durden says about your 'fuckin khakis?' Whether you're in the gym or sparring, whether you're rolling on the mat or running a marathon, you reach that beautiful moment where nothing else matters. You are fully engaged in your current activity. You have achieved flow state. You are living in the moment. You are at peace. *"You're not your job. You're not the money in the bank. You're not your fucking khakis."* Find out who you really are and push yourself to new heights.

If you can find something you truly enjoy doing, you'll find that it is much easier for you to achieve flow state on a regular basis. I have found that having a routine helps you reach this consistently. By tweaking your routine over time, you can realize what is working best for you. It's amazing to watch it all come together.

Now, most people think a routine makes them a slave, when in fact the opposite is true - and yes,

I realize that this sounds counterintuitive. If you simply live "freely" and follow each impulse you have, you're not truly free. You are simply a slave to your base, animalistic desires. Contrarily, if you set out to craft a routine of your own choosing, you're following your higher self's true wants. Short-term this may sound more demanding, but it leads to greater long-term happiness.

For example, despite the struggle of short-term hunger, fasting helps me achieve greater focus for my writing. Perhaps people should stop channeling their inner Hemingway and focus on less food and less booze. You often hear people talk about the physical benefits of fasting and how it will help you lose weight. What is equally important is the mental aspect you can gain from intermittent fasting. By entering starvation mode, your mind grows sharper and this give a laser-like focus to your work. It is as if the mind enters a survival state where you operate more efficiently, increasing focus and determination. It is in this state that I craft my best writing and work most efficiently.

It has taken a long time and great effort to produce a routine that works for me. But all the elements of my routine work together like a well-oiled machine. And this machine pumps out books every year. It creates the energy that leads to Spartan Races and Ultra Marathons. But it didn't happen overnight.

Every 30 days or so, you should take the time to reevaluate your daily routine. Contemplate what is working well, and what is an inefficient use of your time. As time goes on, you will perfect this routine and continually seek more efficient methods for improvement. Also, your mission will change over time, so your daily routine should change to fit each mission.

For instance, those who are training for a marathon will have a significantly different routine than those who are writing a book. Craft the daily tasks necessary to build up to your long-term goals and you will accomplish your mission. By focusing on the day to day tasks, you will transform your goal into a system that will produce real results.

While most people crave freedom, they forget that discipline and freedom are two sides of the same coin. Without discipline, a life of pure freedom is anarchy. It is discipline that creates this life of freedom in the first place, it is discipline that will build a life that will make you happy.

By taking the time to plan out your daily routines, you are freeing yourself from the shackles of impulses. The average person is a slave to their base desires, but they think they're free because they do whatever they want. Throughout their entire life, they are being led by their animalistic desires and hedonistic pleasures. This is no way to go through life.

Those with the Warrior Mindset have taken control of their life. They live intentionally. By crafting a daily routine of their own choosing, they are in control of their destiny.

Craft the Ideal Routine for Your Perfect Week

"A daily routine built on good habits and disciplines separates the most successful among us from everyone else. The routine is exceptionally powerful."

-   *Darren Hardy*

How often does this happen to you? You sit down ready and willing to put in the time and energy to be productive, but you get stuck. You don't know what the best activity is to focus on right now, and you stall out. You overthink and you waste precious time trying to figure out how to best optimize your time.

What if you could skip this frustrating part of your day?

Rather than wandering aimlessly from task to task, you should craft an ideal routine that you can follow each day. You don't have to follow this routine perfectly, but simply creating a general framework will give your life the right amount of order to keep the chaos of daily life at bay.

I create a table with the days of the week on the X axis (top of the table), and the hours of the day on the Y axis (side of the table). Then I write out productive habits that I tend to do at specific times of each day of the week.

For example, I tend to wake up and work out from about 6 to 7. Then from 7 to 9, I'll focus on writing, I even have a couple of time slots set for "free time" or "creative time." This way I don't risk burning out and have dedicated times for me to recharge.

Now, I don't always follow it to the very minute like a robot, but it crafts a framework that I can follow. So, when I am feeling lost in my day, I can easily consult my table and see what activity I'd typically be doing at that given hour. This helps me to stay on task and hold myself accountable when it comes to my daily actions.

These actions seem small when you look at them daily. However, if you can consistently stick with these actions, they begin to add up exponentially over time. The problem is that too many people let their mood or feelings dictate the productivity and direction of their day rather than to develop a system that helps them achieve what they want each day.

I also leave a few hours open for my most productive, deep work. This is the work that produces leads, money or helps me grow my business. For me, the hours are from 9 – 12. These are my most productive hours and I want my most productive hours to be devoted to my most fruitful tasks. This is systematic optimization.

Each day, I set out to knock out 3 daily tasks. Anything that doesn't get done gets added to the list for tomorrow. Every day, you'll have some task that you will regret not doing; rather than dwelling on an unproductive day, simply move that task to your list for tomorrow.

By creating a list a day in advance, you'll save yourself time since you already know what you need to do. When you awake in the morning, you'll awake with a purpose; you will remember how much you wanted or needed to knock out those items on your list and this, as a result, inspires you to get out of bed.

The modern warrior needs a purpose, and too many are living their lives reactively. They wait for the day to attack them and then find themselves worn out, overwhelmed and disappointed with their day. The proactive warrior seeks out his purpose and attacks his day on his terms. This person is driven, motivated and fully of energy.

Plot Your Plan of Attack for the Next Day: DECLARE WAR ON TOMORROW

Every single day is a battle. Good generals plot their attack before the battle has even begun. You need to plan your attack a day in advance.

This gives you a massive advantage over the average person.

Adopt the warrior's mindset and crush your day with this killer routine. Or think critically and adopt one of your own.

12. Seek Voluntary Discomfort

'But neither a bull nor a noble-spirited man comes to be what he is all at once; he must undertake hard winter training, and prepare himself, and not propel himself rashly into what is not appropriate to him'

– Epictetus

There was a popular meme in 2018 on taking cold showers as some sort of lifehack to turn your life around. By 2019 it had largely become a joke as we all knew that taking a cold shower didn't pay the bills. Personally, for me, the idea was a bit silly, but the concept was golden. Don't make a joke about showers and gold.... Ok, moving on. The point is that modern life is so soft, to improve oneself, you must purposefully challenge your mind, body and spirit.

Last year, I started off with a 30-day challenge of not consuming alcohol. Though I don't have a problem with alcoholism, I have found that taking time away from one's typical habits offers great insight into the relationship with said aspect.

Ultimately, I found it to be a great weight loss method. In my 30 days of sobriety, I dropped 7 pounds with minimal changes to my diet, I also realized that in many ways, alcohol is holding me back from greatness. I don't expect to become a teetotaler, but I intend for it to be much less pervasive in my life. And after picking up a few pounds during the holidays, this serves as the perfect counterbalance to that overindulgence.

How Alcohol is Holding You Back in Life

With less alcohol, you see the world so much more clearly. This may be obvious, but if you spend most of your days in an alcoholic haze, then you're going to miss out on huge portions of your life. Even if you're "just buzzed," you're still not fully present.

I also feel way more productive. In the 30 days where I was sober, I added around 6,000 words to this book. I edited and refined my Best of Helm of Awesome book, I was a guest on a new podcast, and I read 5 books.

The effects are undeniable.

Alcohol is the drug of choice for those who prefer to hide from their own problems and anxiety. People will say that alcohol can reduce stress. There's some truth to this as it can make you more comfortable in social situations, boost your mood and help you relax.[8] However, if you abuse this, you can build up a tolerance and make it more difficult to de-stress yourself with alcohol.

Once the alcohol wears off though, you may feel more anxious than you did before.[8] You awake in the morning, scrambling to look through your phone. Did you pull a Rosanne Bar and write a racist tweet? Did you text nonsense to your ex-girlfriend? Or did you only say "I love you, man" to your bros?

The signs of alcohol codependency are: needing a drink to get going in the morning, drinking heavily 4 or more days per week, requiring a drink at every event, and drinking 5 or more alcoholic beverages in one day.

If you can't go 30 days without alcohol, then you are no free man, you are a slave to your desires.

Many people who claim to not be morning people are actually experiencing mini hangovers most mornings. They don't binge drink enough to have a massive hangover that sidelines them for the day, but they drink enough to wake up in a zombie like state. Alcohol is a poison that holds you back from presenting your best self.

Vices are poison to the warrior monk. Be pure in mind, body and spirit.

I honestly feel much better and healthier when I don't overindulge when it comes to alcohol. I rarely wake up groggy. In the past, there would be days where I wasn't hungover, but not 100% with it either. Sobriety has freed me from this lethargy.

What new hobbies could you pick up with all this newfound time and energy? What skills might you learn? Without the excess weight from drinking hundreds of calories, you could become more athletic and energetic. Now, I'm not 100% sober, but I drink significantly less than I once did. Don't let perfect be the enemy of good.

There is a time and a place for drinking, but most of the younger generation are obsessed with drinking for the sake of drinking. It used to be that you would do the work first, then reward yourself with a few drinks. Yet many people today seem intent on partying for the sake of partying.

And there's nothing manly about binge-drinking every weekend. Most guys think it's manly to pound beers all weekend, but then they can't run more than a couple miles or hammer out 25 pushups. The promotion of binge drinking as manly is a marketing ploy to trick young men into handing over their hard-earned cash to giant corporations.

This myth of drinking as an inherently masculine activity is propagated by Hollywood actors who curated the perfect diet and exercise routine for months. They then portray a character who makes drinking look stylish while obscuring the hard work and dedication that led to them looking masculine in the first place. It's the perfect example of a Hollywood illusion.

Since cutting back, I have taken up running as a hobby and I regularly participate in races - everything from 5Ks to Spartan Races. I even ran my first half marathon last year and ran my first ultra-marathon this year. Back in my heavier drinking days, none of this would have been possible.

These 30-day challenges will teach you about yourself, your habits, and the impact these habits have on you. During my divorce, I took a break from gaming. Mostly because I didn't have free time, but also because I wanted to focus on the divorce.

Video Games are Not Real Life

After a lifetime of gaming, I ended up taking a 500-day break from video games. My initial plan was only to stop for 90 days, but I became very accustomed to all the new free time I had to pursue more interesting hobbies. The benefits were abundantly clear to me, which is why the break from gaming lasted so long.

Gaming is a massive time sink and it fuels many negative habits. Now I enjoy gaming, and I even took a few hours to play Vice City over the weekend that I wrote this very chapter, but in that same weekend, I also wrote about 2,500 words in this book, I wrote an email and ran 4 miles on a trail run with some friends. Life is all about balance.

There are many people who hide themselves from the real world. They retreat into their safe space in the virtual world, what they fail to realize is that they are living in a dream world.

There are far better ways for a man to spend his day rather than being holed up in a dark room bathed in the blue light of a screen. This is especially true when literal days' worth of time is being devoted to a single video game. For many people, their default hobby when they have time to kill is gaming. Do you want to spend most of your life staring at a screen at work and then going home to stare at another screen?

As Oscar Wilde says, "Moderation in all things, including moderation." Still you must ask yourself if gaming is making you happy, and more importantly, fulfilled? For many, gaming can become an addiction. So, imagine you gave up gaming. What might your life look like?

It's not unusual for people to spend 10 hours or more in a week playing video games. These same people will tell you that they don't have time for more productive hobbies like reading books, working out or starting their side business.

Gaming offers a false sense of accomplishment that can stunt your personal growth. Though you should really be feeling dissatisfied with the direction of your life, your brain is getting the chemical feedback it needs to feel comfortable with your daily decisions.

Coupled together, alcohol and gaming can be a lethal mix.

Like alcohol, gaming has a way of distorting time. The hours literally fly by without accomplishing anything meaningful. You can spend days sitting on a couch leveling up your fake characters, or you can enter the real world and level up your real life.

Remember, to adopt the warrior's mindset, you must be constantly improving yourself. Are you becoming more proficient with your skillsets? Are you training to be harder to kill?

Procrastination Prevents Excellence

How many great products are you hiding from the world? How many books could you have read if you turned off Netflix? How good would you look naked if you quit playing with your XBOX? How sexy would your girlfriend be if you stopped texting your ex? Quit fucking yourself by delaying greatness.

Every single day you need to write down a list of tasks to accomplish. Aim for three tasks for every day. Use a real notebook and cross them off as you go. When you miss a task, add it to the next day - even if you only get 2 on some days you will see results. Remember, no zero days. Do this EVERY SINGLE DAY for 6 months and you'll be amazed at your accomplishments.

In creating Path to Manliness, I have created a lot of content. I've written two books, have had multiple podcast appearances, lost 30 pounds and have forged powerful connections with other content creators. My first book, Reclaim Your Manhood, is your guidebook to straightening out your life. The information in it is so essential to young men that I priced it as affordably as possible. The eBook is $5 because everyone needs to read this. No excuses.

"Someday" is holding you back. This word is toxic. Your ego will let you use this word to convince yourself that you'll make it big... someday. You'll ask that girl out... someday. You'll write that book... someday. When writing Reclaim Your Manhood, I told myself I wouldn't release it until it was finished, and I kept pushing the release date further and further away. While true, it wasn't finished, I was procrastinating because I didn't feel crunched by this moveable deadline.

After multiple delays, I realized that it would never get done without a firm deadline, so I had to put some pressure on myself. I set a firm deadline and told my followers. Now with some social pressure, I was motivated to write. And write I did. Despite a smooth launch, the last couple weeks were chaos! But it motivated me. It lit a fire under my ass. Most importantly, I published the book and people could finally read it.

You need to hold yourself accountable. Procrastination is the thief of excellence.

You want it to be perfect right? The moment. The book. The website. Whatever the reason behind your procrastination; you're waiting for the perfect conditions. There's an important saying that you need to hammer into your permanent memory.

Don't let perfect be the enemy of good.

Growing up, school teaches us to seek perfection. We are forced to compete for the best scores, perfect answers and perfect attendance. Perfect conditions are the perfect excuse for more procrastination. You don't have an unlimited amount of time on this Earth; you need to use your time wisely and sometimes that means sacrificing perfection for punctuality.

13. Perspectives

"You can rid yourself of many useless things among those that disturb you, for they lie entirely in your imagination; and you will then gain for yourself ample space by comprehending the whole universe in your mind, and by contemplating the eternity of time, and observing the rapid change of every part of everything, how short is the time from birth to dissolution, and the illimitable time before birth as well as the equally boundless time after dissolution."

- *Marcus Aurelius*

By realizing your true place in the universe, you will find that much of the pressure you feel is removed. The truth is, there is so much going on and if you make a huge mistake and feel embarrassed, you should recognize the massive breadth of time itself, and realize, this too shall pass.

When you contemplate the meaning of this, you gain the courage to put yourself out there in the real world and share your work. Why would you let negative energy such as fear and doubt control your path in life?

You must let positive energy guide your life and your work. Focus on the influence your work will have on the world. How might your work help those who need to hear it?

Why do I insist on meditation so often? Because by reflecting on life and contemplating your place in the universe, you can reach those who need guidance. You can share your wisdom and guide those in need.

We get so focused on constant improvement and bettering oneself, that we forget that most people struggle with very basic stuff. When you're an expert in your field, you compare yourself to those who are talking about very advanced ideas and practices. But the average person is completely lost from the very beginning.

The first steps are essential to understand as they are what will be taught to newcomers. Most of which will never have a need to reach these advanced stages. Meaning if you want to become the most interesting man in the world, all you need is a basic understanding of a few subjects, and you'll be more well versed than the average person.

You Have No Idea How Great You Have It

This is why it's good to travel and visit your friends. Talk to them about their problems and any issues they're facing. I recently talked to a guy who was having tax issues and he owes about $2,000 - this is a lot of money for him. I mentioned to him that I owe a lot as well. I didn't specify the amount, but it was $17,000. I could complain about this, and I may already have done, but at the end of the day, I'm fortunate enough to make a good living and be able to come up with this much money. I have another friend who owes even more - somewhere in the six-figure range; it can always be worse.

Keeping things in perspective is how you'll be able to practice gratitude in your life. The average person today has a smartphone that is essentially a modern-day library of Alexandria. The average person has endless entertainment options available to them via streaming services for nearly no cost. The average person has access to so much cheap food all year-round that obesity is an epidemic.

The problems of modern men are not shortages, but rather gluttony. With so much of everything constantly available, the modern warrior must learn to do without through discipline.

Throughout the history of most of mankind, even the wealthiest were starved of such knowledge, food and opportunity. Today, we complain about the difficulties of life when, the greatest difficulty we face is how easy life is.

The 47 Ronin

This is one of the most famous stories in Japanese history. The year is 1701. The place is Japan. Set during the Tokugawa era when

Japan was ruled by the shogun, this is a time where honor was respected above all else. The military elites followed the code of Bushido, or "The Way of the Warrior." Chief among the code of Bushido, was loyalty to one's master and fearlessness in the face of death.

While training in court etiquette, Kira Yoshinaka, a Shogun official grew furious with Samurai Master Asano Naganori of Ako when the gifts he received were deemed inadequate. Asano preached patience, but when Kira called him a "country bumpkin without manners," it was beyond forgiveness. Asano drew his sword and attacked Kira. Asano merely inflicted a superficial would to the shogun's head, but shogunate law is strict in forbidding anyone from drawing a sword in the castle. They demanded Asano commit ritual seppuku suicide.

The death of Asano left the 320 samurai leaderless and impoverished. Their titles were reduced from samurai to Ronin. To not have a master is a great dishonor in samurai culture so they were expected to follow their master in seppuku suicide. Forty-seven of the samurai opted instead to live and wait patiently, while secretly plotting their revenge for the death of their master.

The 47 Ronin swore a secret oath to kill Kira. Expecting such vengeance, Kira posted numerous guards and fortified his home against the 47 Ronin. But they were patient. They waited. They even scattered across the land, pretending to be thieves, mercenaries, even mad men. One of them even went so far as to marry into the family so that he would have access to the blueprints of Kira's mansion.

Their leader, Oishi Yoshio, appearing convincingly as if he had given into decadence and nihilism, began to drink and spent money on prostitutes. He even divorced his wife and sent her and their younger children away to spare them from what they had to do next.

December 14, 1702, 46 Ronin descend upon the castle in the middle of the night as snow falls on the quiet night. One Ronin is assigned to go and tell the tale of their revenge.

Armed with ladders, battering rams and swords, the Ronin surround the house. Simultaneously, Ronin are silently scaling the walls and incapacitating guards who are caught by surprise. As the Ronin attack from both the front and the rear, Kira's samurai awake from their sleep and rush out barefoot to fight the Ronin in the snow.

As the Ronin dispatch the samurai, they see no sight of Kira. They search the house for an hour, finally finding the Shogun official hiding in nothing but his underwear. Oishi offers Kira a short sword, a wakizashi, to commit ritual seppuku. The same short sword the Ronin's leader had used to commit ritual seppuku.

They stare at each other, Oishi on his knees, watching the visibly shaken Kira cowardly refrain from choosing an honorable death. Oishi rises, unsheathes his sword and swiftly beheads Kira.

All 46 Ronin survive their stealth attack, dispatching forty of Kira's samurai. The sun begins to rise as the Ronin walk through town, greeted by cheering crowds. They walk into the Sengakuji Temple, the burial place of their deceased master. Oishi walks up to his master's grave and presents Kira's head.

Despite becoming national heroes to their honor and strict adherence to Bushido, they were charged for their crimes and ordered to commit ritual seppuku suicide. A death more honorable than execution.

On February 4, 1703 as the day turned to nightfall, the forty-six Ronin committed seppuku.

The forty-six Ronin were buried at the Sengkuji Temple in Tokyo, near their deceased master. The site instantly became a site of pilgrimage for many who admired the Ronin for their honor. The forty seventh Ronin was believed to have been pardoned, and after a full life was buried alongside the forty-six Ronin.

Asano's eldest son was returned the title of Samurai, and one tenth of the land was returned to them.

This World is Filled with Propaganda to Warp Your Perspective

The modern-day warrior accepts this truth.

Western man has invested so heavily into capitalism that the decision to produce future generations, is dependent upon the magical line we call the stock market. Our most significant purpose, to procreate, we leave up to market conditions.

Now, even when the market crashes, it often recovers within a few years, and raising a kid is an 18-year long process so why even worry about market conditions?

This is one of those paradoxes where people of lesser intelligence are superior to those of greater intelligence. When you think too much, you become subject to paralysis by analysis. This is true even when deciding on the right time to have kids.

Do you think an ancient Spartan warrior, a Viking or a Ronin would willingly snip their ability to procreate? What greater purpose is there in this life than to create future warriors from your own bloodline? The entire purpose of civilization is to learn from the past so that we may build a brighter future, but many of the brightest are scientifically castrating the future.

An analysis of modern DNA reveals that 8,000 years ago, 17 women reproduced for every one man. This means that throughout much of human history, man struggled to keep his gene pool alive. Yet modern men willfully sacrifice the opportunity to further their genetic lineage in favor of having fur-babies, (a grotesque term for pets) more disposable income and more leisure time.

Rare is it that a man has no option for reproduction in today's day and age. Procreation is far more accessible than in ancient history thanks to marriage and social shame. Men will complain that women only want men who are 6 feet tall, but if this were true, we'd have seen humanity slowly becoming giants.

Ancient Spartans didn't have apps on their phone allowing them to connect with "Hot Spartan Ladies in Your Town." No, they had to work all day in the farm, ride a horse into town and then go find a woman the REAL, old-fashioned way. Some of these men would literally put on their armor, get on an old wooden ship named "Diversity" and cross the Aegean Sea to wage war against other men just for the chance of meeting a nice girl. Yet men today will willfully snip their "manhood" and destroy all chances of creating a future.

People will tell you that fundamentally nothing changes in a man after the snip, but your vet will tell you that your dog will calm down and be more docile after he gets the snip. Apparently, nothing will change except you'll become a nice, domesticated pet - content with your suburban home, minivan and white picket fence. Prozac optional.

Maybe I'm being hyperbolic as this isn't a one to one comparison. They are different procedures intended for different mammals. But you must admit that the ability to procreate is inherently a big piece of what helps a man define his own masculinity.

14. How Failure Makes You A Stronger Warrior

Fail forward by learning from each mistake you make. If you aren't failing, you aren't challenging yourself.

"Everything should be a failure and a success. The failure is typically external, and the success is typically internal."

-   *Sahil Lavingia, Gumroad CEO*

If you're putting your best efforts out there publicly and trying new things, failure is inevitable. The average person sees this as a reason to not take risks. The modern warrior understands the very nature of failure - he understands that through failure, a warrior may grow.

On Becoming Antifragile

A popular new term recently has been making the rounds: antifragility". Coined by Nassim Taleb, antifragility basically takes resiliency to the next level. To be antifragile is to gain from disorder, chaos and volatility. Whereas a resilient person can weather the storm and come out in the same shape as before, the antifragile person becomes stronger. Those who are antifragile are emboldened and motivated through the trials and tribulations they face.

They take failure or the harshness that life throws at them and they use it. They learn from it.

They analyze their weaknesses and strive to become more formidable in the future. The antifragile person is nearly unstoppable. The antifragile person is near invincible as even when they are beaten, they will rise back up. They will come back stronger with each battle they lose.

The antifragile person cares not whether they win or lose the battle, for he will eventually win the war.

Your primary focus is action. Your secondary focus is to learn from your failures. This is the reason why I'm so aggressive in promoting writing. By writing down what you learn, you gain a better understanding of what went wrong and how you can improve yourself going forward.

Rather than let yourself get immobilized by paralysis by analysis, you need to change your mindset with failure. School conditions you to avoid failure at all cost, but sometimes, the greatest ideas come to you through learning experiences of failure.

This is where writing comes into play. When you do fail, rather than letting it get you down. Write down your thoughts on the experience. What went wrong. What caused this to happen? Writing and reflecting on your failures are how you take your life off autopilot and begin to take control of the direction you are going.

From coasting through my 20's I grew complacent in my life. I was the guy with the dadbod who spent his free time watching football, drinking beer and eating chicken wings. I thought I was happy, but I never considered myself to be fulfilled.

Then I went through a tumultuous divorce. When you stand before the family court system that is judging and nitpicking every little aspect of your life, it inspires some soul searching. This led to me busting out of my funk and living a much more optimized life - this was the moment I discovered my antifragility.

Now, I no longer treat my leisure time so nonchalantly. And to quote Henry Rollins, "There is no free time. All you got is go time." I left no aspect of my life free from scrutiny. If I found something superfluous in my life, it was gone. I reinvented myself from the ground up. Now I volunteer at the local martial arts academy to help young kids, I engage in all sorts of local activities to be a part of my community, I wake up bright and early to exercise, I write books, blog posts and inspirational tweets, I created Path to Manliness to inspire other men who are coasting through life to break out of their own funk.

In a strange twist of fate, I now look back upon my divorce with a glimmer of appreciation. While it sucked to weather the storm, there is no denying that the adversity it provided has made me a stronger person. It has given my life new meaning and direction; and now I'm actively engaging in activities that are bettering many people's lives.

Divorce, like many challenging times in life, has given me a newfound perspective on life. Divorce was my moment of antifragility.

While it is easy to start playing the victim when life hands you an unfair hand, there's nothing to gain by doing so. If you want people to feel sorry for you, they likely will, but you'll gain nothing else. There is no profit in the business of victimhood – thinking otherwise is a peasant mentality. You want The Warrior Mindset.

First and foremost, you need to accept that bad things will happen to you, and they have likely already happened. Acknowledge this. Mourn if you must - but then you'll need to find a way to move on with your life.

The difference between resilience and antifragility here is whether you decide to learn from this adversity. If you merely survive through the storm, you are resilient; but if you can look back at what happened for lessons and implement them into your life, you have become antifragile.

Writing down these life lessons allows you to keep a short memory of your failures. You can get them off your mind and lighten your load. But you also retain the important lessons learned allowing you to transcend past resilience and into anti-fragility.

While you shouldn't actively avoid failure, you shouldn't seek it out either. You can insulate yourself from the biggest failures by taking small risks. If the risk could wipe you out completely, then it is almost never worth it. Even with a small risk, the stakes are simply too high.

Also be sure to build in a plan for failure. If these events are predictable, become anti-fragile by preparing for them. Too many people ignore knowable risks because they think they can dispassionately respond as they happen. Why would you intentionally want to be reactive when you can be proactive about it. Create backup plans so that you can immediately respond to failure.

-   If you rely on social media for your work, then create backup accounts or use multiple platforms to hedge your risk.
-   If you have essential data saved on your laptop, back it up regularly to the cloud or another location.
-   If you have a single customer who is responsible for a disproportionate

percentage of your income, seek to build up existing customers or find new ones.

As you make mistakes and learn from them. Create a set of rules to live by. These rules will grow over time and learning experiences. By sticking to these rules, you'll find that you can often lower your risks and stick to your own criteria. Rules help you stop shooting by the hip, bringing intention and order to the chaos of your life.

When you put all of this together, you create an environment that allows for you take calculable risks. If you fail, you have contingencies set up already. If something predictable goes wrong, you can skip the "Oh shit!" phase and move on to solving the problem.

I once had a boss who perfectly embodied the idea of skipping the "Oh shit!" phase. This man was the perfect leader as he was hard working and deeply invested in his work. Yet he never let his emotions guide him, even when facing catastrophic failure. And his calm demeanor was not only inspirational but reassuring.

He did this by responding to failures, chaos and other problems by simply thinking or asking, "How do we solve this?" or "What can we do about this?" He completely skipped the "Oh shit!" phase. And many years later this has stuck with me.

"The only man who never makes mistakes is the man who never does anything."

- Theodore Roosevelt

15. The Bear Necessities

"Retreat into your inner sanctuary. Here, away from strain and distraction, you are free to observe the world and your reactions objectively."

- *Marcus Aurelius*

I do this every day and it is where my greatest ideas and thoughts originate.

Stripping Down to the Bare Necessities Shows You Who You Are.

Modern life is so full of distractions and noise that it is a challenge to find peace. Today it is a constant struggle to quieten all the noise and just sit still and listen. To look inward and think deeply. As time goes on, the distractions and noise are only getting worse.

Buddhist monks have simplified their lives by removing all unnecessary material goods. All their possessions will usually fit in a small backpack. This quiet and simple life frees them from the noise and struggle of typical western life. These Buddhist monks will wake up early to meditate for 1 to 3 hours and they'll meditate again at night.

Meditation completely rewires your brain to help relieve stress and improve overall physical health. According to a study from UCLA, long-term meditators have more grey matter volume throughout the brain than non-meditators.[12] Even a few days of meditation will help you to improve your focus and memory; it has even been shown to reduce anxiety and aid those with social anxiety disorder.

I consider meditation such a worthy practice for the modern warrior. The more time you spend intentionally seeking quiet, the more natural it will feel for you to seek peace and quiet. The more time you spend in quiet solitude, the better the understanding of yourself you will.

I am reminded of how great it is to simplify one's life whenever I stay in a hotel. There is great power in being stripped down to the bare necessities, it allows you to focus on the task at hand. It provides a great opportunity for peaceful meditation, I feel most like myself in the simplicity of a hotel room. My luggage is simple and light.

Stripping down to the bare necessities really reminds you of who you are.

There is an old Zen story about a Zen Master named Ryokan. He lived the simplest life in a small hut at the foot of a mountain. Then, one evening a thief visited Ryokan's hut but was dismayed when there was nothing to steal.

Ryokan returned to find the thief standing in his home. "You may have come a long way to visit me and you should not return emptyhanded. Please take my clothes as a gift."

Not sure how to react at first, the thief took the clothes and left the Zen Master.

Ryokan sat in his humble abode, naked, watching the moon. "Poor fellow, I wish I could give him this beautiful moon."

You can't steal the moon.

You likely forget this. So many put their sense of self-worth in their material goods. They define themselves by their social status and worse, they let others define them by this as well.

The car you drive, the clothes you wear, the job you work... none of that is truly who you are. And deep down you know this truth.

All of that physical stuff is fleeting. Cars break down. Clothes wear out. Jobs disappear. But none of these small tragedies will ever change who you are. This means they are ultimately meaningless.

If you truly want to know yourself, and everyone should know thyself, then do this.

Sit down in a simple room without distractions. Leave your phone in another room. No TV. No music. Nothing. Just you. Grab a notebook and a pen and start writing. Write down your thoughts, your goals, your beliefs. Whatever you want. You may even enter a state of stream of conscious writing where thoughts flow naturally from mind to paper.

Make this into a daily ritual and you'll learn more about yourself than you ever thought possible. This gives you power. This gives you purpose. This gives you confidence. People notice and respect a man (or woman) who knows himself (herself).

I'll leave you with a poem from Zen Master Ryokan...

My hut lies in the middle of a dense forest;

Every year the green ivy grows longer.

No news of the affairs of men,

Only the occasional song of a woodcutter.

The sun shines and I mend my robe;

The moon shines and I read Buddhist poems.

I have nothing to report my friends.

If you want to find the meaning, stop chasing after so many things.

- Ryokan

16. Craft Your Principles to Guide Your Life

A man who hasn't designed his own set of guiding principles is a man who is at the mercy of his base impulses, or worse, another man's principles.

"An important place to begin in philosophy is this: a clear perception of one's own ruling principle."

- *Epictetus*

Modern man is under a constant assault from influences outside of his control. It is undeniable that narrative warfare is being waged against traditional masculinity. They want you to be weak – but I want you to be strong. This makes me "problematic", this makes my book difficult to market with traditional avenues.

Pop culture, cultural reinforcement and advertising campaigns are a constant assault on masculinity. The end game being for corporations to create better marketing targets. They know to sell a product, you really sell an emotion, and women are better customers by and large than men. What the world doesn't want you to know is that a happy and fulfilled man doesn't need to buy into the lies of materialism. Adopt the warrior's mindset and be a stoic man who favors minimalism.

Some of these outside influences are positive such as reading from The Meditations or motivational speakers. Even social media can be a positive influence on your life with the right curated feed. You'll find that these more positive influences are much more difficult to find than the more decadent and thus, more profitable influences.

There are many negative influences in your life. Influences such as advertisers who aim to make you fat, feminine and soft. This is to make you more malleable and easier for advertisers to market to. The infotainment news companies seek to divide you and keep living in fear - even if they trade their political pundits like baseball players. Remember, red or blue, they all bleed green.

It is highly profitable for these major corporations to keep you a weak and obedient slave. Overly processed foods are highly profitable, but they'll turn you into a fat and lethargic blob of a man. Outrage generates clicks and those who write the news will gladly sell their souls for advertiser dollars at the expense of your emotional well-being.

In fact, most of what is fake is profitable and pushed down your throat daily. So, whenever you find yourself getting angered at the TV, the headline of the article you share but don't read or the outrageous commercial, do this; ask yourself, cui bono? That's Latin for "who benefits?"

You'll often find that it's not idealism shaping the narrative, but profit. And your outrage is only fueling the outrage industrial complex.

So, What's a Man to Do?

One must set out to create his own guiding principles so that he may be able to think critically.

Also consider all the media you consume. Now in the 280 characters allotted on Twitter, I spout off about quitting video games, the news and sports so that you can go live like a monk. In your newly found monastery, you may contemplate the perfect tweet to write each day. But we can't all be monks. Hell, most of us don't even want to live such a life.

But you do need to sit down and consider what principles do you live by? If you haven't read Uncommon Mentality by Logocentrifugal, I recommend it.

I used one of his tools in this book to physically write out my own principles. They're on a piece of paper in my desk now. Soon it will be framed on the wall where I will be reminded of what I stand for daily.

In my earlier chapter, The 7 Pillars of Masculinity, I talk about authenticity. This is an essential trait today, hence it being the first pillar.

1. Be Authentic – In all forms of expression, be authentic. This means being true to oneself.

This is a difficult pillar to uphold when there are a plethora of forces out there trying to shape you into something that you're not. If you don't have a well-defined set of principles, you are even more easily shaped.

Be true to yourself, and you will be more resilient to the forces that influence you. This is one of the secrets of the real world. Those who seek to control you don't want you to be yourself, they don't want you to be unique, they don't want you to be strong. You must be mindful of the media you consume. Be mindful of your friends. Be mindful of your thoughts.

What you think, you say. What you say, you do. What you do, defines your character.

If you're reading this though, you're not like everyone else. You have consciously sought to better yourself and set yourself apart. So why are you still living like you're one of the average people in society?

I encourage you to think critically and live life according to your own personally crafted set of guiding principles. These principles are your rock. Your anchor. Your core tenets that guide you through your life. They are essential to your very being. Treat them with respect.

A man without principles is a puppet to a more powerful man who cultivated his own set of principles. It is these principles that make a man stand out in a sea of weak followers who blindly do what they are told.

Now, no one is their best every day. And there are times when you may be in the wrong frame of mind. But if you have a set of rules memorized and engrained in your head, then you have your stability. Even on these days of weakness, you are reminded to live according to your own ideals. Ideals that were created when you were at your best.

Most people don't want to take the time and energy to craft their own rules or principles. They merely borrow them from someone else. If your principles are not your own, you are at the mercy of another man or the ideology made by another.

Think about what changes would make you into the ideal person you want to be. How would that person live their life? What defines them as a person?

What daily actions do you need to take to embody this?

What motivates them to get up in the morning?

What drives them to push themselves harder than their peers?

What reason do they have to live such a disciplined life?

Write it down and this will serve as a constant reminder of who you are striving to be. We are all works of progress. It is in this way that you are a work of art.

17. Seek Solitude and Achieve Flow State

"Retreat into your inner sanctuary. Here, away from strain and distraction, you are free to observe the world and your reactions objectively."

- *Marcus Aurelius*

Modern life is fraught with distraction from noise, notifications and an ever-increasing amount of stimulus. To be able to achieve flow state, you need to learn self-control and the ability to enter a deep focused state.

Flow state is that mindset whereby your mind can enter an effortless state of focus on what you are working on. It is difficult to achieve but worth all the effort. By cultivating a routine that minimizes distraction and stimulus you can achieve these flow states with greater ease.

It is in these flow states where deep work is possible. This is how you create your greatest works. If you can create times in your schedule where you achieve these flow states, you will produce your greatest achievements.

So How Do You Achieve Flow State?
Your phone is one of your greatest tools for networking, researching and sharing your work, but ultimately it is also your greatest distraction

from achieving flow state. Therefore, the best of your writing will come from pen and paper. Sometimes the simplest solution is the most effective.

This means you will need to create an environment and a routine that will separate you from as many of the distractions as physically possible. This may even mean keeping your phone turned off or in another room.

Your phone is an alarm clock skinner box. What's a skinner box? BF Skinner put rats in a cage and offered the rats a reward at varying intervals.[15] He discovered that the rats became more attentive and interested when the rewards would arrive at random times. This is true with humans too. This is evident with casino slot machines or more recently, with loot boxes found in modern gaming.

Casino gambling techniques are being used in video games that are marketed to adults and kids alike. This will one day either become illegal or at the very least rate games as "adult only". Video game loot boxes are where you can spend real world money to buy in game content that is randomly generated. It's essentially a lottery ticket designed to hook players into spending more money. What is particularly insidious is that the odds of winning are obscured in the game code.

Like Skinner's experiment with the rats, these loot boxes are designed to keep players addicted and coming back with more money. And since you don't know what you're going to get with each loot box, you get a boost of dopamine when you finally unlock one of the better items, no matter how much money you spent to get it.

Gaming used to be a mindless escape for people, created by artists who wanted to create great games. Now they use psychological tactics to make even mundane games addicting. Phone games will tempt you to login every single day so that you get these unlockables that are completely worthless.

Your phone is unpredictable and is causing you to feel anxious. When you get that notifications or text, you get an initial burst of dopamine - which is why social media is so addictive. If you get more likes than you were expecting, you get a reward from the social bonding area of your brain; but if you don't get enough, you're disappointed.

Social media is the binge snacking of the virtual world. You aren't ever truly happy when you get virtual social acceptance. So, you want more. You'll find yourself working harder to get the dopamine you once got, putting yourself in an addictive habit of continually seeking out more social acceptance in the form of likes.

In our increasingly digital world, what we truly want is a real sense of belonging. This digital acceptance is a mere derivative of what millennia of genetic encoding craves. Due to the nature of social media likes, they naturally provide a reward at random intervals and in random quantities. This leads to humans returning to the source of the reward more frequently, just like the rats.

When you get that craving to check up on your social media, ask yourself whether or not this is helpful to you in the long run. Is it time sensitive? Are there more important areas of your life that you're neglecting?

So often, I'll find myself drifting in and out of awareness. The distraction of the phone can cause me to miss more beautiful moments in the real world - or more dangerous moments. Today, 14% of fatal car crashes involve cell phone use. In 2018, this amounted to 4,637 people.[9]

The modern warrior needs to constantly be aware of his surroundings. If you're too busy staring at tweets on your phone, you're susceptible to an attack or other life hazards.

Take time during the day to distance yourself from it so your mind may get a reprieve. This allows you to enter flow state with greater ease. Achieve this by leaving your phone in another room. It is in these moments of uninterrupted deep work that you'll achieve your most important accomplishments.

Even when you don't mind being bothered, your phone is constantly interrupting you. Rather than letting your phone boss you around all day with pings and buzzes, turn off as many notifications as possible. Set aside a time in the day for you to check important items such as email or less important items like social media. Man was not meant to be interrupted all day and it is making you less productive, more anxious and less happy.

Learn to Enjoy the Quiet Moments

You should find time for solitude every day. I do, and it is where my greatest ideas and thoughts originate from. When I am walking alone in the wooded hills in my backyard or along a serene trail the chaos of life begins to seem insignificant. Simply sitting quietly away from outside stimuli can lead to a more peaceful and healthy life.

Most people are very uncomfortable being by themselves or even doing normal tasks by themselves. This is a sign that they are unhappy with their own self-image or uncomfortable confronting their own thoughts. As we learned earlier, voluntary discomfort is part of the natural process of improvement.

Learn to embrace the quiet and acknowledge your own thoughts. This is often a challenge for people who are used to the constant noise of daily life. This is where meditation will grow your mind like a muscle. Through the implementation of meditation into your daily routine, you are growing this muscle. In time, meditation becomes natural and even enjoyable.

Seeking solitude also allows you to center yourself and achieve focus in your life.

It is in these quiet moments that you can contemplate thoughts you have, ideas you heard or simply embracing the quiet. Through daily practice over time, seeking solitude can help you learn to love yourself.

One place of solitude I find is when I put my headphones on, play some inspiring music and go for a run. As my mind is reaching a meditative state, amazing thoughts and ideas can percolate in my mind. In fact, many great ideas for books, blog posts and more originate while I'm outside running 10+ miles. And in this state, you can reach the mythical runner's high.

The modern-day warrior poet recognizes the balance between the physical and the mental. By sharpening your mind, you can hone your body. By strengthening your body, you are strengthening your mind. The two are inextricably linked and help to reinforce each other. In balance, you will find you are more effective and powerful.

This concept of seeking quiet is the key to the future. Every time you shift your attention, you force your brain to reorient itself. In the land of mass distraction, the disciplined man is king.

Learn to do deep uninterrupted work and you will be a superhero.

18. Find Your Tribe

Finding Inspiration from Your Brotherhood

Forge a tribe of strong and motivated men and you'll increase your ability to survive, to grow and to reach more like-minded individuals.

A man is an independent creature, seeking to do everything by himself because we are taught to believe that there is strength in independence. Hollywood and video games hammer this point into the minds of young men where the lone hero saves the day against impossible odds. While being independently capable is a strength, mankind has thrived in the strength of tribalism.

By forging a tribe, you're benefiting from the shared skillsets of your brothers. They will hold you accountable when you begin to slip up. And you'll be able to support one another if you or a brother needs temporary help.

In fact, this isn't as foreign of a concept as you might first think. These types of groups have existed throughout all of humanity. Today, you have a plethora of men's groups to consider joining:

- Church groups
- Shooting / hunting clubs
- Survival groups

- Running clubs
- Freemasons
- Business networks
- Golf clubs (heh)
- Gym partners
- Spartan / obstacle course teams
- Recreational sports teams

Society won't want men to group together in these clubs for there is power in numbers. Those at the top of the pyramid don't want to see social change, they don't want to see men forming powerful tribes as they might one day begin to change the social order through empowering each other.

The Benefits of Forming a Tribe

What few men understand is that you aren't alone in searching for your brotherhood. People who share your ideology and mission are also searching for you. They too are frustrated by the problems in their life. They too are looking for a connection. They'll be just as inspired and motivated from meeting you.

We all get burnt out at work after spending long hours chasing the dollar. That is why we need to take a vacation from time to time. When you come back, you find yourself refreshed and your boss finds a more productive worker; I have found this to be true as a writer as well.

Seeking a weekend retreat with fellow writers is more effective than a vacation though. Why is that? Because you feed off the energy of fellow writers. You gain insight into the brilliant minds of your brothers. Best of all, the amazing conversations that flow with each glass of whiskey plant the seeds for so many new topics to write about. In the days since returning from my latest trip to a cabin in the mountains of North Carolina, I have written thousands of words.

In the weeks leading up to this weekend retreat, I had been tirelessly working on this book, but I hit a wall. Normally I can add about 500 words a day to the book I'm working on, but I had been struggling to add 50 words a day during this period. Since this writers' retreat to the soaring snow topped mountains of North Carolina, I found the inspiration and the motivation to write more meaningful words for this book. Now I know it is on pace to becoming a worthy successor to its predecessor Reclaim Your Manhood.

Through networking with others online, you can gain unprecedented advantages. You'll have a sense of comradery, support and true accountability. The future will reward those who understand the power of leveraging connections made online.

In my time online, I've been able to forge a brotherhood with many great men. By connecting, I've been able to share advice, struggles and ideas with other brilliant minds. And in this retreat, conversations were focused on self-mastery, systems to write better and of course plenty of laughter. Coming back from this trip, I found myself refreshed and full of so many writing ideas that I had to grab my wooden 'Path to Manliness' pen and start jotting down all of these ideas in my notebook before they escaped my mind.

The rise of the internet has made it easier than ever to connect with your fellow men. The problem is that too many are content to stop at a superficial online relationship. While this is better than doing nothing, it is no replacement for a flesh and blood, real life interaction. Conversations are better offline. And once your return to the online world, that online relationship will be that much stronger and will hold more meaning.

Insulating Your Tribe from Opposing Threats

A man alone is like a soldier without support. He can make an impact on the world, but he will always be limited by logistics, by narrow ideas and by lack of support when he is under fire. When you have a brotherhood working with you, supporting you, and encouraging you, well then you become akin to a platoon - now you are a force to be reckoned with, now you will draw the attention of a much larger audience.

With that larger audience will come enemies, and they'll be more formidable. You'll find there will be those who will try and infiltrate your group, elements will attempt to sabotage you and your mission. There will be weak crabs in the bucket that will try and tear you down.

These enemies will study your tribe in silence. They'll wait for the opportune moment to strike and see if they can find holes in the armor. They'll look to see if there are weak links to tear your tribe apart. And if you haven't done a good job strengthening and supporting your tribe, you may find it splintering by opposing forces.

When forging your tribe, think of building it in concentric circles where there will be layers between the inner circle and the outside world. Before allowing an unknown element into your group, watch them and see how they interact. Then consult your fellow tribe members to gain their opinion. Is there something you missed? Everyone looks at people differently and by getting multiple sets of eyes on each person, you are further insulating yourself from a potential spy, an enemy or an outright psycho. All of which will happen to you if your tribe grows large enough.

Once you and your inner circle have decided that you have a potential candidate, bring him into the outermost layer. This will likely not be a real-world place. This may be an online forum or a secret group chat. The point is to make it appear as if the candidate is past the vetting process so that he will feel comfortable enough to show his true personality and potential flaws. This allows for your current tribe to interact with your new recruit and to gauge his worthiness and his motives.

No one is perfect but these flaws will appear more obvious now that your candidate is speaking more candidly. Pay attention and take note of what you see.

- How does your new potential tribe member respond to criticism?
- Does he take it in stride or is he obstinate?
- Does he get angry over petty quarrels or does he diffuse a situation?
- How does he interact with women?

When dealing with people online, you'll find there are some guys who simply don't know how to talk to a woman like a normal person. This will be a problem if you have women in your tribe.

It is essential that your group has a proper vetting process, that the team work together to defend one another, your brotherhood will need a code to live by. All of you have an inherent responsibility to live up to the code yourself, and most importantly to ensure the rest of your tribe lives up to the code.

Secret Alliances and Espionage

What do you do if someone is trying to infiltrate your group for nefarious purposes? There is a fine line between trying to understand the purpose and mission of your tribe versus gathering intel on various high-ranking members. And the differences can be subtle. As your tribe grows more influential, you will find rival tribes may grow jealous or malicious of your success.

- Are you insulated against such attacks?
- Have you even considered that this may happen?
- Is it happening right now without your knowledge?

I have firsthand knowledge that there are many people online gathering dirt on various high-level individuals online. Narrative warfare has become a force to be reckoned with. The online world can have powerful real-world implication if you understand how to effectively wield a narrative. I have seen not only the aftereffects of con men being exposed but I have also seen behind the scenes of people gathering intel with the intent of creating an ace up their sleeves.

If you notice this happening, it's best not to reveal everything you know right away. It is often advantageous to subtly move this person away from the more important discussions. It's best to leave them wondering why they have been pushed out of the inner circle. Citing "creative differences" or claiming you are going in different directions will lead to a smaller chance of creating negative side effects. The fly in the ointment will be left with a degree of doubt over why he was cast out.

Secret Alliances and World War I

Social media is much akin to the real world circa World War I. If you're not a history buff, let me explain; there were a few very large players in the world such as the British Empire and the Ottoman Empire - this was painfully obvious to even the most normal people of the time.

What was much less obvious was all the secret alliances going on behind closed doors. Before the world broke out into World War I, Britain, France, Ireland and Russia created an alliance called the Triple Entente. Simultaneously, Germany and Austria-Hungary formed the Central Powers alliance.

So, when Serbian terrorist group, The Black Hand, assassinated Archduke Franz Ferdinand, heir to the throne of Austria-Hungary, they threatened war on Serbia. Shortly after, they made good on their threats and declared war on Serbia. Germany sided with Austria-Hungary and secretly Germany feared war with Russia was inevitable. Russia sided with Serbia and feared war, so they mobilized. Germany saw this as a threat and when Russia refused the German ultimatum to demobilize, they declared war on Russia.

Germany then decided to attack France but made the mistake of invading Belgium en route to France. Britain had a secret alliance with Belgium and immediately declared war on Germany. So, thanks to all these secret alliances, a small regional conflict exploded into a full-blown World War resulting in the deaths of an estimated 21 million people.

This roundabout point illustrates how many players online have their own secret alliances and allegiances to various groups and people. Now, I'm not telling you to self-censor or hold back your opinion. What I am saying is to not attack another group of people without your own tribe in your back pocket and only then, do so twhen there is something to be gained. You simply don't know what you don't know, and you may be getting involved with much more than you initially believed. The wise warrior does his research before making his move.

Go out and find your tribe. Go out and save the world.

19. What is the Path to Freedom?

Are you living a life of freedom or are you a slave to your base instincts? Think about your average day. You wake up, probably after hitting snooze a few times. You grab your phone and check your email, or Fakebook, or stare at some ass on Instagram. Wasting time in bed so later you can complain that there isn't enough time in the day to pursue more meaningful pursuits.

Or.... You decide to wake up early feeling rested because you were disciplined enough to go to bed early. You do some light stretching and get in a quick workout to help wake up. I'm writing this section after running 5 miles at the gym and weight training for my next Spartan Race. What are you doing with your time on this Earth?

Life is too short for the snooze button. Wake up with a zest for life and do something you enjoy first thing in the morning. The anticipation of an enjoyable activity will encourage you to get out of bed faster. Change up your morning routine with one of these ideas:

- Keep a book by your bed and read when you wake
- Start with an exercise routine
- Listen to a music playlist that pumps you up

Personally, I start my days by exercising while watching the Joe Rogan Experience. Not only is this an activity that I look forward to, but it is also one that benefits me on multiple levels.

Don't let yourself become another NPC who rambles about the weather and complains about the same boring topics: "Ramble Trump... ramble so tired... ramble how about <insert celebrity gossip> LOL emoji...

The average person seems remarkably content living a wildly mediocre existence. Once you begin to surround yourself with more motivated people who pursue a life of purpose, it is near impossible to even stomach the ramblings of those who have no interest in pursuing a more meaningful life.

Instead of merely surviving, aim higher. Spend time meditating deeply on philosophy, on life, on your aspirations. When you talk with people, be genuine and skip canned conversations. Go deeper and find a true connection with your fellow man, or woman.

After you finish your morning routine, you rush through breakfast and get some caffeine somewhere. Probably a sugar filled mess of a drink that is only making you fatter and hurting your self-esteem. I know this is a common issue because the line at my typical Starbucks is usually so long that it backs up into the nearby street.

You fight traffic to get to work where you probably spend half your day reading some fool's blog or mindlessly scrolling through social media rather than putting in real productive work. Most of us are so distracted or disinterested in our daily work that we actively seek out distractions. Why is this? Because we tire of slaving away for someone else's mission.

Therefore, you must look inward and seek out your own mission. One that is worthy of your interest, of your time, of your energy. The secret to finding your own mission is that you'll likely end up spending more time than a 9 to 5 would require. Why work so hard? Because when it is your mission, you will care.

After work, you rush home, fighting traffic again, so that you can watch some more Netflix. You eat a big dinner and self-medicate with alcohol or nicotine to numb yourself because how else can you get through the daily grind?

You watch the news which is divisive and negative. And yet, none of this even gets our attention because we are constantly staring at our phones throughout the day. How can we resist since the notifications and messages constantly remind us that we might miss something important? Though it rarely ever is worth our time. Is this how you want to live your life?

Look Inward and Seek a Greater Purpose

After finishing a test in high school, I found myself unprepared for a philosophical question on an English test: "What do you hope to accomplish in your life?" I sat in my desk chair and stared down the question, deep in thought, finally challenged.

I wrote "To build something that lasts longer than me." Its haunted me to this day. The idea of our mortality haunts all of mankind, it's what drives us to strive for more than mere survival. Humanity has lost touch with our primal nature. We now find ourselves striving for meaning in a world without struggle.

How much time do you take for self-reflection? Do you meditate on the day or ponder new projects that you are working on? Do you open up to anyone about what you are really feeling, or do you simply regurgitate what you heard elsewhere? Some days I feel like we are speaking only in memes and emojis. Few people have the courage to take off the mask and reveal honest thoughts and speak authentically.

Do you fear the judgment of your friends and family? If you seek the approval of others, you will always be a slave. That is how the matrix traps you. It traps you into fitting into a preordained set of rules. Get a standard job, buy a safe car and don't take risks. What if something goes wrong? Most "safe" jobs have you living paycheck to paycheck and one hiccup could spell a disaster.

Don't worry. There are so many cheap distractions to help you forget about these truths. Society encourages you to stay in your safe space of Netflix, alcohol, video games and more.

I encourage you to step outside of this formulaic and programmed lifestyle. Start writing and become more mindful in your actions. Learn to think critically. You will have people in your life doubt you when you take risks. These risks you take will make them question their own lives and that makes people uncomfortable. People tend to resist change.

Live a life authentic to your true self. Don't tell your friends or family what you are planning to do for they will only doubt you as they doubt themselves. Rather show them what you have done after the fact: action speaks volumes and will shut down the doubters. Once you have real results to show for your actions, you'll be undeniable.

Throughout most of my twenties, I felt lost. I feared getting trapped into this lifestyle that has become the standard for so many young men. They are trapped or stuck in a rut. They want to live a good life but are lost. Some call this a quarter life crisis. I was never warned or prepared for such an existential crisis.

College conditions young people to follow already beaten paths. Women pressure men into settling down with the white picket fence and a big heavy mortgage. With the debt of 30 years of mortgage payments, taking risks become nearly unthinkable. You find yourself physically and spiritually stuck. Is it any wonder that so many young people today are rebelling against the lives their parents lived?

For decades, the millennials grew up watching sitcoms and cartoons like the Simpsons, showing us the misery that can come with the so-called American Dream. Marriage, a big house in the suburbs, expensive cars and a boat. Are these things making us happy or more neurotic and anxious? The American Dream comes at a hefty cost. Debt. And debt equals slavery.

While the eighties and nineties brought extravagance and opulence of an economic boom, the millennials were deprived of this world. We were constantly shocked with crushing opposition. We watched old CRT television sets wheeled into classrooms where we witnessed skyscrapers collapse. We watched jobs vanish in the financial collapse brought about by greed and corruption and followed with bailouts rather that swift justice.

The American dream is an elusive concept for young people.

This life is full of people who will tell you the best way to live. Make sure that you understand what it is you want in this life.

"A man who procrastinates in his choosing will inevitably have his choice made for him by circumstance."

- *Hunter S. Thompson*

Which is why I encourage you to start writing. Writing is the key to breaking your chains.

By writing, you will gain insights into your mind, into your frustrations and ultimately into what your mission is in life. You know you have ideas and goals, but they are lofty. By writing them down, they become grounded. The next step is to set a deadline.

A goal without a deadline in merely a dream. Set a deadline and make it reality.

- Do you want to run a Spartan Race? Sign up today.
- Do you want to write a book? Come up with a title and put it up for preorder.
- Do you want to start a business? Start working on marketable skills and make an offer, or a product that you can sell.

Whatever you want to do, you need a deadline to crush the voice inside of you that encourages procrastination. Now you have discipline. Now you have meaning. Now you have a path to freedom.

How is this freedom, you ask? Simple. You want this. You said you did. Look, you even wrote it down. Probably in pen. And you can't erase pen, so you're stuck doing what you want. Deal with it.

If you didn't stick with this and did whatever you felt like, would that be freedom? No. Society tricks you into thinking impulsivity is freedom because it makes you easily swayed by advertisers - realistically, it would make you a slave.

Think about what you hear on TV. It's full of terrible advice that sounds vaguely appealing because it appeals to your desires. Those with simple minds are constantly falling prey to these tired tactics. Buy this new car! Don't worry about the 5-8 years of payments. Get a loan! Don't look at the interest rates. Buy overly processed junk food, but don't look up the health effects. You need to go to this college. Don't look up to see whether it's accredited... If you follow every impulse and do whatever you want, you are a slave to your impulses.

While most people crave freedom, they forget that discipline and freedom are two sides of the same coin. Without discipline, a life of pure freedom is anarchy. It is discipline that creates this life of freedom in the first place.

Along with discipline comes a schedule or routine that builds over time. Those who consistently work towards their mission, are successful in turning their dreams to reality. No zero days. Don't break the X! Every day is a battle and you need to declare war.

Take your newly formed habits and stick with them. Leverage your routine to conquer each day, and you'll be amazed by the results. You'll wonder how you wasted so much time. It's not that you were lazy or didn't care. You simply didn't know the best way to attack your life. You didn't understand the warrior mindset.

Set goals. Set deadlines. Stick with it. Be disciplined. Be free.

Do this for 6 months and you'll be amazed at the results.

Discipline is the path to freedom. This sounds paradoxical which is why freedom is so elusive.

20. The Law of Diminishing Returns

"Moderation is good, in moderation."

- *Oscar Wilde*

With alcohol the first drink is good, the rest is downhill.

With video games, a short break is fun, but hours a day lead to a wasted life.

With food, the first bite is tasty. Eventually this becomes compulsive and addictive.

Control your impulses or become a slave to dopamine.

Discipline is the path to freedom.

Many men, young men especially, are trapped in a dichotomy mindset. Does a real man do this or that? Is this alpha or beta behavior? Should I go 100% traditional conservative or be a total manwhore? This is a childish mentality.

Never is this more apparent than with social media, where brevity is king. This is the problem with the microwave mindset that so many have today. Most discussions now, whether online, or a political debate are forced to turn a more nuanced discussion into a brief soundbite. This leads to the dichotomy mindset.

As a boy becomes a man and gains more real-life experience, he begins to realize that the world is rarely so black and white. That the reality of the world favors moderation found in the gray between black and white. Even those of the most extreme idealism can find an exception that proves the rule they believe in so intently.

This is difficult to convey when we are being conditioned to have a microwave mindset. The mainstream media makes a living off the 10 second soundbite. So, if you can't concisely make your point, they'll frame a point to their liking. This leaves little room for nuance. Social media is built to reward short term content.

One of the great qualities of Twitter is the 280-character limit which makes each tweet easily digestible. You expect more of your followers to read it than they would read your long form media. The barrier to entry is low enough to accommodate those who lack a decent attention span. The problem with this is that most tweets are lacking in nuance due to this character limit.

This is evident in the comments of most viral tweets. There will always be someone with too much time on his hands to tell you all the exceptions to what you said. These people often miss the point entirely. They'd rather poke holes in an argument than see if they can gain some wisdom. They are too fixated on showcasing their intellect due to their own insecurities.

Don't fixate on the minute details or exceptions here. Instead, focus your attention on what the writer is trying to convey. Forget the exceptions.

They are beside the point. Consider the impact the writer's words can have on your life.

The truth often lies somewhere in between. While you'll always have die-hards, who claim no life has room for sports or games, and that a "real man" stops fooling around with childish nonsense; if you look for the more nuanced answer, all work and no play makes Jack a dull boy. Those who don't take time for breaks will burnout. Balance in all things.

Of course, the opposite is true, hence why you'll hear self-improvement gurus tell you to stop wasting so much time on social media, video games and sports. Because for most people, their problems are wasting too much time on play, not burning out from too much work.

The reason why people get so upset when gurus attack their hobbies: sports, video games or whatever, is because they recognize they waste too much time on these pastimes. People are quick to defend their addictions. This is their ego talking.

We are often prone to suffer from our own cognitive bias. If you want to find information stating that gaming is a positive aspect of your life, you'll select the information that fits your own bias.

For example, gaming is a huge time sink for most people. Yet, gamers will ignore this truth while focusing on the positive aspects. You can say that you meet friends through gaming, but that ignores the fact that you sink so much time into the habit - if you quit, or simply cut back on this time, what would your life look like?

Would you find more time for exercise, eating better and socializing in the real world? Again, this is all about the law of diminishing return. A 30-minute break spent gaming is fun. But if you end up gaming until 3 A.M. and losing sleep over it, then are you better off "relaxing?"

I often will give out free advice in my writing to all who will listen. I'm grateful for the engagement but often frustrated at the plethora of men who struggle to see nuance in these words.

For example, I often will rail against the obsession of the almighty sportsball, which is a catchall for all popular sports. Now those who read my more nuanced blog posts and emails will realize that when I say quit wasting your time with sportsball, I'm not demanding pure abstinence from watching sports. In fact, I still enjoy the occasional game and I always enjoy a good UFC fight, but neither rule my life.

I have achieved balance. This message is for the guy who is so caught up in "his teams" progress that he spends more time and energy following the achievements of other men than his own achievements. This is not a fulfilling lifestyle. If you know the on base percentage of your favorite baseball players better than you understand your own personal budget, your life is out of balance.

Watching the occasional game is fun. Letting your weekend get ruined over a ball game is not. This is base tribalism because you need a sense of belonging. But these sports tribes are superficial in nature. The games are trivial, yet some adults take it too seriously.

True tribes are formed through participation in activities, not passively watching others engage in activities. If you need to feel that you belong, find a group of men who share a common interest with you. Through competition or actively engaging in hobbies, you'll form significantly stronger bonds.

Alcohol and sports often go hand in hand, which I've always found paradoxical. You don't see athletes drinking beers to supplement their workouts, do you? Yet, this is what the advertisers have led you to believe.

If you drink an average of one beer a day, that adds up to 73,000 calories a year. That's 20 pounds in beer alone every year. And how many of you drink more than 7 beers on weekends alone? This is why you can't lose weight.

Alcohol is tricky because it can be an entirely different beast for each person. For you, abstinence may be the only answer - and this wouldn't be such a bad thing. Without the distraction of alcohol and its effects, your productivity should go way up.

Like most things though, it's all about the law of diminishing returns. One beer every now and again isn't going to hurt most of you. It's the nights where you take it too far, binge drinking beer after beer that lead to poor decisions, hangovers and wasted days.

Modern society has a strange relationship with alcohol. Largely due to its pervasiveness in our culture and media, we tend to forget that it's a drug. Even though, as far as drugs go, it tends to be one of the more deadly drugs.

On the Independent Scientific Committee on Drugs (ISCD) alcohol scores a 72, which puts it at the most harmful drug on this scale.[10]

21. Break Your Chains

"So often times it happens that we live our lives in chains and we never even know we have the key."

- *The Eagles, Already Gone*

What are you afraid of? Are you still living a life that was chosen for you by your parents? By your education? By your media habits? Do you truly know who you are? What echo chamber are you imprisoned by?

If these very simple questions make you uncomfortable, then you've got some deep soul searching to do. Rest assured, it's not too late, but time is fleeting. *Tempus fugit.*

You need to come up with a set of guiding principles to govern your life. I'll bet they never taught you that at school. And I'm damn sure they didn't teach you how to create your list of principles; I covered this in Chapter 15, Craft Your Principles to Guide Your Life.

This set of principles makes you a more resilient warrior. A warrior without a purpose is merely a mercenary, capable of being swayed to whoever wields a modicum of power. But a man with principles is a man of honor and integrity. In the land of distraction, this is becoming a rare man.

Sadly, most men live their lives as mercenaries rather than idealist warriors. This means they are slaves to their debt or lust for materialism. Most of these men will claim that they must work a job they hate to support their family, but upon closer inspection, you'll find oversized McMansions, overpriced cars and a lavish lifestyle.

The trap of materialism is one that enslaves many and is a leading culprit in causing men who live lives of quiet desperation. This is often a life sentence. Even as people make career advancements and increase their income, they let their expense rise right along with it. This is called the "lifestyle creep".

Downsizing this lifestyle may be inconvenient, but if it comes with peace of mind, isn't it worth it?

Now I'm not claiming that you should quit your job today merely because you're unhappy, but you don't have to stay there forever. Take some of that time spent on Netflix or video games and begin working on your passion, your project. In a couple years' time you may find you have built up a sizeable side income. This could even grow into your full-time job if you dedicate your time and energy to it.

This isn't necessarily about the income either. You surely have a hobby that you can focus on, this could become your sense of purpose. Whether you create a blog, or a group, or a full-blown side business, this can be a source of networking with others who share your passion. We all need more meaningful connections based on shared interests.

Even worse, many are slaves to the opinions of others. Rather than to pursue their own deep desires, they'd rather repress these wants in favor of chasing a more respectable job. How many authors, artists and other creative types chose a more traditional life out of fear for what others may think of them? How strange to be more concerned with what others think of you than what you think of yourself. Ironically, the secret is that most people think much more of themselves than others.

Too many spend their entire lives waiting for that one day when the conditions are perfect. One day, you'll be lying on your death bed, and you'll start reflecting on your life. How are you going to feel about the actions you took today? Are you going to be fulfilled and happy with the life you led?

Or are you stuck chasing the American Dream? The average American sees themselves as temporarily embarrassed millionaires. These are the ones who will lambast the poor even while they themselves are poor - classic ego defense. Rather than to admit that they are struggling, they claim that they'll be wealthy one day, and will even vote as if they already are.

Each day the American dream becomes more and more elusive. Though it's not impossible, the barriers to entry are tougher. Traditional methods of accessing the American Dream fail to yield the fruitful results that our parents and grandparents were afforded. The path of simply getting a degree no longer guarantees success, but rather crushing debt. That being said, the right degree can still lead to a successful life.

Today, pursuing the American Dream will lead you down a path of crippling debt. You think this isn't drafted by design? This sets you up to be a slave to our capitalist system. You'll be stuck working for the rest of your life to pay off the debt of your degree, the debt of your mortgage and the debt of your car. And you can bet your ass as soon as you start getting ahead and paying down these debts, you'll find forces at play encouraging you to take on more debt.

How many people do you know who fall into this trap for their entire lives? They are more numerous than you know. Your neighbor who just bought that shiny new SUV to replace his older ride that ran just fine? He's addicted to chasing the shiny. He wants to trade his freedom for more material possessions. You might be alarmed if you saw how much debt is weighing on his shoulders so that he can flex on his neighbors to feign success.

Your friend who got a big promotion and raise that just sold his house? Well he would have had more cash to stash away ensuring an early retirement, but he'd rather tack on more debt with a bigger house he didn't even need. These people are addicted to debt and will never be free. They worship the American Dream as their God. They believe that they will keep making more money and never even consider getting fired, getting laid off, or their company going under. Hell, even State Farm lays people off. Bear Stearns collapsed. How long do you think your job will exist? Forever?

True Creativity is Authentic

It takes resilience to get through this life and remain true to ourselves. Fear and doubt are the enemies of creativity. It is unfortunate that school plays a large part in instilling those fears and doubts that steal creativity from this world. How many great content creators has the world been robbed of because of an outdated school system that means to crush your spirit?

There are a lot of great teachers working very hard for much less pay than they deserve. For the most part, this school system is not their fault. I am placing the blame on the school structure and on the classmates. Unfortunately, the typical school day is set up to stimulate methodical and left-brain behaviors while depriving the right-brain where creativity thrives. That is because capitalism favors left-brain since it makes for a more productive society. School has never been designed to create unique minds that produce innovative products or ideas. It has always been about creating obedient workers and compliant citizens.

Classmates, through peer pressure, make it very difficult for a young mind to express itself in sincerely. Growing up is fraught with challenges and awkwardness and letting your freak flag fly is risking chastisement or even ostracism from your tribe. It is through this peer pressure that the school system can self-enforce the rules.

I wish I could state that this childish behavior ends with graduation, but for most, it follows us into adulthood. We live in a time where our values are truly out of alignment.

It is weird to decide to quit a high paying job for a life of wanderlust or less stress. It is normal to work longer hours to get that promotion, even if it means missing your kid's little league game.

It is normal to become a vegetarian because you care about animal welfare, but it is odd if you decide to raise your own animals for eggs or meat.

It is unacceptable to smoke a natural plant that is found in nature, but a drug dealer in a white coat is free to give out synthetic drugs produced in a lab and treat the American public as guinea pigs.

Life is stranger than fiction, and too many of us take it all at face value. The way we live our lives is not natural and it prevents many from obtaining happiness. We should feel free to become who we are meant to be.

We need to learn to consume less and create more.

We need a reason to get up in the morning, a passion. Hopefully it is your job, but maybe it is a side project for now. Everything you do should be about making that passion become a reality. Though it is hard work, it is the means to a fulfilling life.

"All things find fulfillment in actualizing their nature. You needn't seek anything else. If you pin your happiness on anything beyond this, you can't be free – you will be a slave to that which you desire."

- *Marcus Aurelius*

Go Out in the Real World and Be the Hero Your Community Needs

It's better to admire the man in the mirror than the woman in the past. The greatest warriors don't allow a woman from their past to corrupt their future, yet many men are so paralyzed by an old flame that they can't move on with their lives. Learn the lessons of this book and you can begin to love yourself. Learn to let go. It is time to move forward with your life.

Most wars you fight in your life will last longer than you expect. This is the great filter for success in life. Those who continue long after most people give up are the ones that life rewards with success. The simple truth is that if you can outlast the competition, you'll likely find success. The mere thought of having to work for years is enough to deter many from ever even starting. These people who give up too soon would rather spend a few months chasing one idea, then chasing a different idea when that get rich quick scheme fails. They'll do this unsuccessfully for years.

The simple formula of taking action, persisting through adversity, and adjusting your tactics will take you farther in life than any get rich quick scheme. But most people don't want to hear that it takes hard work. Most people don't want to accept that it will take time. This is a tough sell, but that's how you know it works.

I am constantly watching people struggle to do too many things in their life. I see this with parents who overwhelm their kids with too many activities. I see this with adults who want everything. I see this with online marketing where people attempt to be the jack of all trades, yet they master none.

Take a good hard look at your life and start paying attention to what is working. The areas of your life that are producing results, those are the areas you need to double down in. The areas of your life where you're struggling or outright failing, cut them out or minimize the time you spend on them.

There's a lot of people out there who complain about the state of the world today. And they'll tell you about it online, but that doesn't change the world. It's simply easier to make a post complaining on social media than to present a solution. Real change happens in the real world.

The number one way you can shape the future of masculinity is to get out in the real world and show the young generation a positive image. So, put down the Xbox controller, take a break from the online forums and go out into the real world and interact with real people.

One of the best places is by coaching or assisting with young men or boys. This can be done with sports, church youth groups or volunteering with at risk youth. You can leave a powerful impression and help shape the future.

Think back to your youth. How many coaches left a positive impact on your life? How many life lessons did they teach you?

It is imperative that young men and boys grow up with a positive view of masculinity and a positive self-image. Get involved so you can make a difference in their lives. By becoming a positive influence, you can help shape the future of mankind and leave your mark on this world.

This may require you to step up your personal game though. You may need to get back in shape, to dress better and to act assertive and confident. It is never too late to change your life. What can you do today to improve yourself? Be persistent and disciplined with this change and you won't recognize yourself in a year's time.

The greatest problem facing modern society is the lack of positive male role models in young men. We have witnessed the rise of father figures like Jordan Peterson who teach kids how to become responsible adults. When advice like "Make your bed" is considered profound, it paints a picture of a void in these young men's lives.

You too can help young men and boys. You have gained great wisdom and knowledge through your years. Help share what you know. After reading this book, realize that you are well ahead of the average person who spends most of their time playing video games and eating

Doritos. Simply showing a better path can make a huge impact.

This advice is worthless if you only read it. You must now implement it into your daily life. This book is your reminder that you now have the mindset of a warrior. Use this power wisely and responsibly.

Go out in the real world and be the hero your community needs.

Ryan Felman

About the Author

Most people fear failure, but I have learned to embrace my own failures. While most will run from these devastating events, I've learned from my biggest failures. It is when life has me beaten to my lowest moments that I find the strength and resolve to better myself. Failure shapes you into a stronger person, if only you listen to what it's telling you.

I've crashed cars, been divorced and been on academic probation. The secret to life is realizing that failure will set back everyone. Especially successful people. If you have the strength inside of you to withstand these blows, then you will only come back stronger.

I have authored two books now with this one and Reclaim Your Manhood. I've authored multiple eBooks on Social Media Marketing and Brand Management. I have also learned how to build websites and successfully drive traffic to them.

As a resident of gorgeous Tennessee, the woods and the mountains have inspired creativity and a penchant for writing in me. When I'm not writing, I am spending my time with my family, running obstacle course races like Spartan and instructing Tae Kwon Do.

For more information about Ryan Felman and your very own Path to Manliness, visit me online at:

www.PathToManliness.com

If you enjoyed this book, please write me a review to help this book reach more young men.

Sources

1. http://www.winternightsfestival.com/viki ngnorse-values/
2. The Templars and the Assassins, James Wasserman, p 105
3. *Eddé, Anne-Marie (2003). Vauchez, André, ed. "Assassins". Encyclopedia of the Middle Ages. Oxford. ISBN 9780227679319.*
4. *Nowell, Charles E. (1947). "The Old Man of the Mountain". Speculum. 22*
5. *Frampton, John (1929). The Most Noble and Famous Travels of Marco Polo.*
6. *Acosta, Benjamin (2012). "Assassins". In Stanton, Andrea L.; Ramsamy, Edward. Cultural Sociology of the Middle East, Asia, and Africa: An Encyclopedia. Sage. p. 21. Retrieved October 13, 2015.*
7. *Hodgson, Marshall G. S. (2005). The Secret Order of Assassins: The Struggle of the Early Nizârî Ismâʿîlîs Against the Islamic World. Philadelphia: University of Pennsylvania Press. ISBN 978-0-8122-1916-6. Retrieved September 15, 2010.*
8. https://www.healthline.com/health/alcoh ol-and-anxiety
9. https://www.thezebra.com/texting-and-driving-statistics/
10. https://www.verywellmind.com/alcohol-is-the-most-harmful-drug-3969483
11. https://www.globalbreath.org/mindfulnes s-coaching
12. https://www.forbes.com/sites/alicegwalto n/2015/02/09/7-ways-meditation-can-actually-change-the-brain/

13. https://nces.ed.gov/programs/digest/d16/tables/dt16_303.70.asp
14. https://www.psychologytoday.com/us/blog/sleep-newzzz/201805/what-you-need-know-about-magnesium-and-your-sleep
15. https://www.smithsonianmag.com/science-nature/bf-skinner-the-man-who-taught-pigeons-to-play-ping-pong-and-rats-to-pull-levers-5363946/
16. https://www.realclearpolitics.com/2018/02/27/of_27_deadliest_mass_shooters_26_of_them_were_fatherless_435596.html
17. https://owlcation.com/social-sciences/Psychological-Effects-On-Men-Growing-Up-Without-A-Father

Thank you for reading The Warriors Mindset: How to Become the Modern Warrior

Thank you Oceane, @MadameMarketing for editing my words into a piece of beauty. Your work has made this into a professional work.

Thank you to Garrett Dailey, @Libera_Rex for his amazing graphic design work on the cover.

Ryan Felman

Adopt the Warrior Mindset

Made in the USA
Columbia, SC
29 July 2021

42618553R00119